Raku
Pottery

Robert Piepenburg

Raku Pottery

Pebble Press
Farmington Hills, Michigan

To Shanna

The translation of the Rikyu poem is from *Cha-No-Yu The Japanese Tea Ceremony* by A. L. Sadler. Used by permission of Charles E. Tuttle Co., Inc., Tokyo.

Copyright © 1994 by Robert Piepenburg
First edition published 1972 by Macmillan Publishing Co., Inc.
866 Third Avenue, New York, N.Y. 10022
Latest revised edition published by Pebble Press, 1994
24723 Westmoreland, Farmington Hills, MI 48336–1963

Publisher's Cataloging in Publication Data
Piepenburg, Robert, 1941–
    Raku, philosophy / Contemporary techniques.
    1. Raku pottery.   I. Title
NK4340.R3 1991   738.1
ISBN: 0–9628481–1–5

Library of Congress Catalog Card Number: 94–66587

jacket cover
Jeff Mincham, Neoteric Vessel, 14" high
frontispiece
Robert Piepenburg, Black Point—Sea Ranch Series, 8" high

Printed in the United States of America

Contents

ACKNOWLEDGMENT

Though I did not fully realize or acknowledge her special contribution in the beginning, I am extremely grateful to my editor Constance Schrader for her generous and professional assistance. Her skill and personal counsel was invaluable to the being of this book. With particular gratitude I am thankful to Christy Bartlett, Director of the Urasenke Foundation in San Francisco, for her time and wisdom while going over the material on tea. Also I want to express my appreciation and thanks to Susan Nordlinger and Wendy Piepenburg for their professional production assistance. Last, but by no means least, I again thank all of those ceramicists who expanded the scope of this book through their gracious cooperation.

Foreword

AS A POTTER...

Many potters, and I include myself among them, find it easy to function in the world of mute arts; but in the scholar's or poet's world of verbal arts, we become ill at ease. In teaching pottery I am aware of speech as a vehicle for communication, and the fact that it is difficult to find the right words to express those usually unspoken feelings of relatedness that working with clay can produce and extend.

If I am to be a good midwife, as teacher and author, I must enter into a dialogue with meanings felt and meaning expression. As a teacher it is easy to explain and demonstrate ceramic techniques. But when it comes to the more subtle areas of personal development and individual involvement, I must hope propinquity will awaken student perceptions. Because the reader cannot be with me in the classroom or studio, and we cannot work together and exchange rhythms, ideas, and a "sense of life," I will have to try to verbally clarify the dualism between the nonverbal and the verbal.

Spoken words are sounds; written words are pictures or symbols that name, describe, or explain concepts and objects. Ultimately, words separate; they are objects describing still more objects. Nonverbal communication is a direct experience, an experience where subject and object are united, without mediator, on the bridge of the senses. Words are experienced in a linear fashion, but pottery is total and simultaneous in its impact.

Potting is more than technique; it is more than the forming of clay and the making of objects. It is, in many ways, the forming of the self. I do not know to what extent we become aware of our selves through daily activities. I have never before labored to define, examine, or bring this awareness from a preconscious to a conscious level. I have only felt it— sometimes fleetingly, sometimes passionately. I have tried to define and develop my own thinking—to enunciate how potting is in my life. Just as you might unroll a scroll to see its entire surface, writing *Raku Pottery* has helped me to unroll my thoughts and lay them out where I can disclose myself to myself. Hopefully it will be of some help to you also.

An inquiry into the essence of life is part of Zen Buddhist philosophy. It is no accident that raku developed with the growth of the Japanese tea ceremony, an aspect of Zen. Zen has never made a distinction in the arts; a poem, a drawing, a pot, or a musical arrangement are equally beautiful. And a good pot is no more accidental than a good poem.

Raku comes from a background of universal human experience and offers potters spiritual insight into themselves as well as their craft. As potters, we can only hope to widen our consciousness so that our work can have a deeper meaning. Working with clay can often satisfy an inner need. I know a woman who was a professional painter until she had a child; afterward, she could no longer work on a two-dimensional canvas and turned to pottery where she felt in touch with a life-giving substance.

I have noticed very sincere and sensitive potters examining my work. They quietly look inside the piece, turn it over, inspect the foot, follow the glaze, and then carefully return the pot to rest. I often sense that they are looking for some insights into the maker. With their minds attuned to their senses they scrutinize the exposed and the hidden identity of the maker and try to touch his feelings and personality. When they succeed nothing is concealed—least of all my pleasure at the moment. Others will examine a pot not for any insight into its maker, but in terms of its form, size, texture, and, most of all, color. They do not understand that it reflects human experience, they are looking for something to fill an aesthetic or functional need. Raku is a poor choice for casseroles and makes leaky flower vases; it is pottery that is apart from a utilitarian function. Raku must be approached with a different criterion in mind.

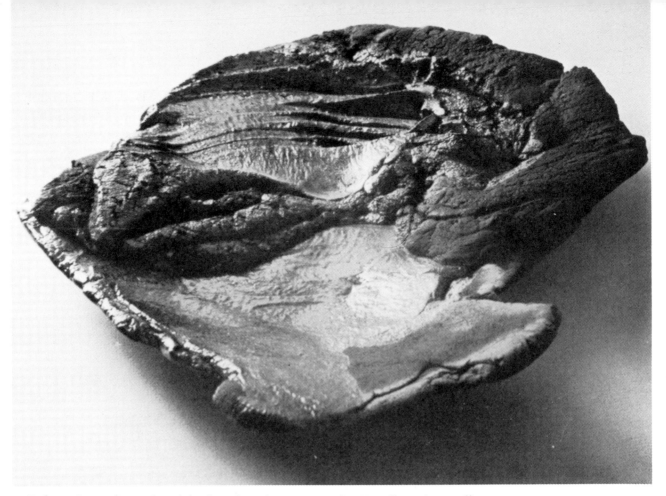

Robert Piepenburg, hand built raku plate 18″ wide. To allow for wall mounting, holes were made on the underside of the piece with a bent section of brazing rod.

If someone were to ask me why I, as a potter, like a particular piece of pottery, I might reply that when I look at the pot, I see an aspect of myself shared and reflected by the potter. As I become more involved in pottery, I experience myself more fully, and I am better able to understand and appreciate the experiences of others. Usually, I do not like a pot because of some lack of rapport. My approval of a pot is partially dependent on my understanding of its artist, but more so to the extent that I have experienced the same intuitions the artist is trying to express. There is, however, no absolute scale.

Our work represents us. It reflects our vision and spirit. It echoes our moods and experiences. Pottery is not created by the hands alone but by the entire body and being. It is not unusual to describe pottery in human terms, to speak of a thin lip, a narrow neck, a rounded shoulder, a tumescent belly, a masculine form, a feminine form, or even a tear of glaze—to use terms such as whimpering, timid, sensual, pretentious, or sophisticated. In China the T'ang potters regarded the unglazed foot of a pot as being naked, and thereby without concealment of its maker. I think an intuitive approach to reviewing and evaluating pottery is far more honest than a dealer's cold-blooded pricing or a collector's acquisitory analysis. Pots express an intimacy and can impart the qualities we value in people.

Our pottery gives testimony to ourselves. To a potter, education is really self-education; it is the continual revelation of oneself by oneself. Each time the potter transforms a mass of clay the clay is transforming the potter; the creating is the searching and finding of meaning; an attempt to unite man and his being. I often believe that a beautiful pot achieves that goal.

It is very difficult to sell or give away a beautiful pot. They should be kept around, if not as reminders of the enlightenment they provide, then for their expression of a moment. But, if they are to break or be given away, we must remember that they are really impermanent objects and have their immortality in their creator and the visions that evolved in him during the fever of their birth.

A potter must continue to search for his or her own meaning. The act of preparing the clay by mixing and wedging is not as important as the act of preparing ourselves. We want to know what we are going to produce with the clay and with ourselves. Like a bud growing from a stem and reaching for the eternal light of the sun, the potter sets at his wheel with both clay and being "on center," knowing that, as one opens and pulls up the spinning clay, growth will take place for the clay and for the potter. If the clay form were to mature only to wobble and collapse, a change would still have occurred within the potter.

A question often asked is, What is the distinction that separates pottery from ceramic sculpture? Ceramic sculpture has an integral life of its own. It is concerned with exploring and creating new or different areas of artistic communication and expression. Often is is created by either a subtractive or additive process (the subtraction or addition of material such as clay, metal, or plastic). Pottery is growth by evolution—the potter generally creates by molding clay from one shape to another. Whether or not this is a valid distinction is really unimportant to the potter or the sculptor. What is of relevance is the transformation of *self* that takes place during the engagement with the clay. The potter is like the clay, and is formed by development and evolution.

The Zen precept of growth is that yielding contributes to strength, and resistance contributes to weakness. If this philosophy is applied in the studio to the clay and the potter, the strength of both will remain in the pot. The potter and the pot are like many living things in nature. The process of inner growth is the process of life. The concatenation of the seed, the tree, and the fruit are like the pot and the potter—they grow from the center. The concrescence that takes place between pot and potter defies analysis; the spirit flows between the form and its maker.

The skills and techniques of the potter are decisive only in that they must be mastered until they are intuitive; they must be assimilated, be part of the center, to be effective. They serve as vehicles for feelings and creation. The potter, like the dancer, cannot be freely responsive to the moment until he or she has mastered and subordinated the techniques of the disciplines. Students often become overly enthusiastic about the process of throwing and make a whole raft of dull, lifeless pots. Technique alone does not provide the substance and the vitality of life. There are times when I feel complete but leave the potter's wheel tired and unhappy. At other times I approach the wheel sensing frustration and find the clay pulling me together. There are times when the clay and potter are at odds, when the potter struggles with his or her own identity through the clay, but these unproductive sessions are more than compensated for by those precious moments when the potter and clay are in harmony.

The harmonious dialogue between pot and potter during the stages of conception is what gives pottery life and spirit. For this life-spirit to exist the potter must give all of himself; and it is in the act of giving that love resides.

R.P.

Raku Pottery

*David Roberts, tall coil built bottle, burnished and carbonised raku,
24" high.*

1

Raku
In Japan

A DESCRIPTION AND HISTORY

To fully understand raku, we cannot embrace one phase but must look for a kinship with all its phases. One way of defining raku, other than as a type of pottery preferred by Japanese tea masters, is to say that it is a low-temperature technique of firing porous, low bisque fired pottery, usually bearing a lead glaze. The technique generally involves a placement of pottery in a pre-heated kiln with tongs and removal from the kiln, again with tongs, while the pot is still glowing hot.

One story explaining the introduction of tongs into the raku firing process centers around one of Japan's many natural disasters. During the frenzied rebuilding, Korean potters in Japan were called on to produce enormous quantities of roof tile. In their haste, they began to use tongs to remove the still-hot tiles from the kiln, and discovered that the tiles did not crack or break. The clay's ability to withstand this shocking move from the hot kiln to the cool air was attributed to the high sand content in the clay. Japanese potters had long since claimed most of the good clay deposits, forcing the Koreans to work sub-standard clay containing large proportions of sand. It is known that earthenware clay bodies were used exactly as they came from the natural clay deposits and it is very possible that a raku clay body may have been discovered in this way.

Tea Bowls

With the exception of a few contemporary potters, the raku clay pottery of Japan, particularly the tea bowls, are usually hand-built pieces. The hand building of raku is traditional; raku was valued and favored for its tasteful unpretentiousness which is associated with and achieved by hand building. The history of raku goes back almost four hundred years, but even today there are Japanese potters who wheel form tea bowls and then hand form the same bowl when the clay is leather hard. This hand forming encouraged the valued irregularity of shape.

Tea bowls are seldom made perfectly round. They are usually designed to conform to being held in both hands, since that is the way they are normally held when they are used for drinking tea. To achieve this some potters take the not quite dry, leather-hard bowls and gently toss them into the air catching them in both hands. The top edges of the

Graciela Bustos, slab construction, 5" × 11" in diameter.

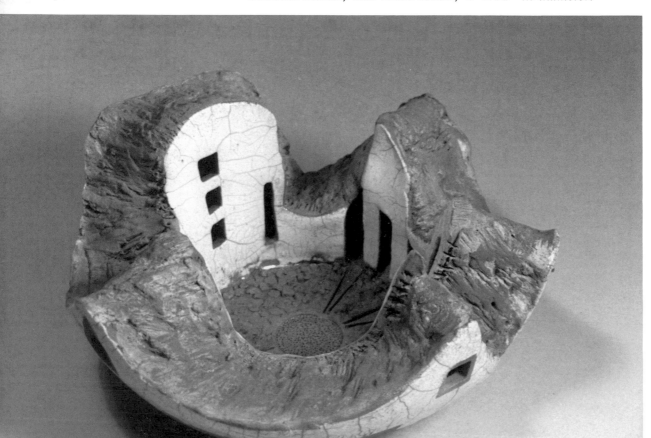

Kathy Sowa, form with porcupine quills, 10" × 17" in diameter.

bowls are undulating so that the rims feel pleasant to the lips when the bowls are held to the mouth. The base of the bowls are usually left unglazed exposing the clay from which the bowl was made. The only decoration, except for the soft thick glaze, is the interplay of the natural colors and contours. The shapes of raku tea bowls are infinite. The shorter, flatter bowls with large surface diameters cool the tea and are used in the summer; the taller bowls with smaller rim diameters are usually used in the winter to retard the rapid cooling of the tea.

Hand-made raku bowls are often formed from a lump of clay that is pushed, pulled, and worked by the fingers into a crude-looking mug shape. When leather hard, the form is then held upside down, and a footrim is

Joe Zajac, Solar Stone Panel, two part wall sculpture, 2 1/2" x 12" x 46".

Black raku tea bowl named Tamamushi, *"Golden Beetle"; bears the seal of Donyu, the most famous member of the Raku family (early Edo period). It is 3³/₈" high and 5" in diameter.*

carved from the thick base with a bamboo knife. The carving is done by using as few knife strokes as possible; the footrim is often made from only one stroke of the knife. It is the aim of the potter to put the essence of one's entire being into the forming of the foot. The knife marks and the foot are prized because it is said that the maker of the bowl can be understood through these marks.

A Short History

No one knows exactly how and where the use of lead glazes and tongs first developed in the firing of raku. Lead glazes were used in Egypt and Persia as long ago as 500 B.C. In Japan, low-fired earthenware with lead glaze was made in the government kilns at Nara for use in the imperial court in the seventh century A.D. It is not known if tongs were used for removing this ceramic ware from the kiln. In form and color the green-and-white lead-glazed Nara ware resembled the ware of the Chinese T'ang Dynasty, and pieces were frequently mistaken for Chinese imports. In the twelfth century the use of lead glazes had disappeared in Japan and they did not reappear until the sixteenth century.

Historical Periods Relevant to the Study of Eastern Ceramics

Japanese	Chinese
Nara (645–794 A.D.)	T'ang Dynasty (618–908 A.D.)
Heian (794–1185 A.D.)	Sung Dynasty (960–1127 A.D.)
Kamakura (1185–1392 A.D.)	
Early Muromachi (1392–1395 A.D.)	Ming Dynasty (1369–1644 A.D.)
Late Muromachi (1395–1573 A.D.)	
Momoyama (1573–1614 A.D.)	
Edo (1614–1868 A.D.)	
Meiji (1868–1920 A.D.)	

Because the Japanese government did not adopt the Western calendar until after the Meiji era, some discrepancies exist between the Western and early Japanese lunar calendar. China did not adopt the Gregorian calendar until the year 1912.

Judy Wieneke, extruded sculpture form, 10½" high.

Steve Olszewski, flat bowl with textured top, 4" × 14" diameter.

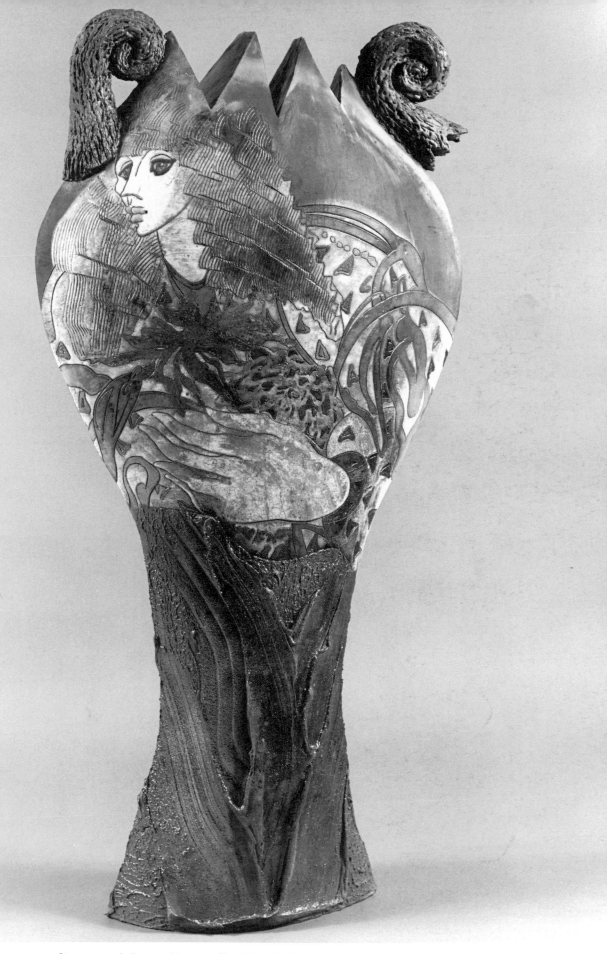

Steven and Susan Kemenyffy, The Ending, 8″ × 24″ × 48″.

The history of pottery in Japan is obscure. Ceramics was a local enterprise and there are no written records and few artifacts. Japan, like many countries of the east, went through periods of centralized authority and through periods of feudal rule. The Nara period and the later Heian period were times of central imperial power, and there was much Chinese influence and a lively commercial exchange between Japan and China.

During the Heian period, the central government began to crumble and the ruling power in Japan passed from the regency of the imperial family to a military government whose capital was in Kamakura. During the feudal Kamakura period loyalty and obligations of the local lords were linked to military strongmen. In this respect the period was somewhat comparable to that of Europe during the Middle Ages. Barons and lords held territory but were forced to pay tribute to military overlords (shogun) and the emperor, who was even more remote. A system of checks and balances maintained some stability and control over military conflict. However, Japan was not a unified country—it was a group of small principalities held together by military and political alliances.

During the Heian period (794–1185 A.D.), there was little progress in Japanese ceramics. Official relations with China were severed and the knowledge of Chinese pottery and glazes was lost. This was tragic since some of the loveliest pieces of Chinese ceramics were produced during this period. Porcelain was developed at this time by the Chinese, although it did not reach its zenith until the Ming Dynasty. Japanese ceramics declined, and lacquerware became popular. The Japanese almost lost interest in ceramics. The widespread popularity and use of lacquer is frequently given as a reason for the late development of their pottery.

The Japanese aristocracy of the Kamakura and Muromachi periods between the twelfth and the sixteenth centuries were importing ceramics of the Sung Dynasty, and the Sung influence can be seen on the Seto ware of that time. The real influence of the Chinese on the growth of native Japanese ceramics did not occur until about the fifteenth century when official trade was reopened with Ming China, and large quantities of Chinese ceramics were imported. This pottery was immediately prized by the feudal and military lords and appreciation of ceramics reached a new level. The introduction of Chinese ceramics was such a stimulus to the Japanese that by the end of the Muromachi period the products of several Japanese kilns were beginning to reflect a new energy and a vigorous new growth; at the same time Chinese pottery and ceramic ware had reached its last flowering.

Maurice Grossman, Moon Dog, 7″ × 16″ × 25″.

Zen Buddhism and the Way of Tea

During the Muromachi period, pottery was not the only Chinese art that was popular and appreciated in Japan. The drinking of tea, which was closely associated with Zen Buddhism, developed into a ceremony and led to new vistas of human consciousness and expression—particularly in pottery.

In seeking these new vistas, we must remember that each of us is a special being with a unique spirit. If we are not alert to ourselves we will be unable to realize the spirit that is in each of us and we will be unable to accept the spirit and meanings of raku. The tea ceremony with the help of raku tea bowls was used to span the gap between spirit and embodiment in Japan.

Buddhism originated in India during the sixth century B.C. It later emerged in China and was adopted in Japan. Buddhism reached great heights in India during the third century A.D.; it later died out in India, but it had been brought to Ceylon, Burma, Tibet, China, and Japan. Various sects and movements have emergd from Buddhism. Zen Buddhism, one of these sects, became very active and strong in Japan.

As early as the Nara period (645–794 A.D.), the Japanese were importing tea from China. In the year 729, Emperor Shōmu Tenno ceremonially served powdered tea at his palace to over one hundred Buddhist monks after they had chanted the Sutras. One of the monks is said to have gone on and built forty temples, each with tea shrubs in its gardens. Later, in 1191 A.D., a monk brought Sung tea seeds from China and planted them near Kyoto, in the Uji district. Tea that was cultivated in Uji was used for ceremonial purposes and it is still thought by many to be the best green tea in the world.

By the end of the fourteenth century, tea drinking had spread from the Zen monasteries to the aristocracy where tea identification contests were held. Prizes were given for correctly identifying the types of leaves used and the districts from which the leaves originated. The prizes were often lavish—a house and servants for life. Two hundred years later, owing to the patronage of the shogun Ashikaga Yoshimasa, tea drinking became an independent and secular ceremony. During this time, empha-

Graciela Bustos, Gate of Civilization, deeply carved wall relief cut into sections for firing and mounted on 3/4" plywood with Franklin Titebond construction adhesive, 1¼"×43"×45".

sis was placed on the beauty and rareness of the tea vessels, the skill of the tea connoisseurs and the decor of the tearooms.

Murata Shuko (1423–1502 A.D.) is considered the founder of the Japanese tea ceremony; he established a new philosophy for the drinking of tea. This philosophy was based on spiritual accord. Shuko sought a spiritual relationship between host and guest. Rank and status were forgotten during the ritual of the tea ceremony.

When Shuko was a young priest he was asked to leave the temple because he kept falling asleep. A doctor prescribed tea as a stimulant for him, and he began drinking tea and serving it to his friends. When the shogun, Yoshimasa, heard of this, he ordered Shuko to arrange a ceremony for the drinking of tea. Although special etiquette was already in use, Shuko set new rules for tea drinking and organized the formal tea ceremony. He became the first Tea Master in Japan. Shuko devoted himself to the art of drinking and serving tea, and tea flourished. Jo-o,

This untitled work from Patrick S. Crabb's Shard Plate series measures 3" x 18" x 20". It was slab constructed over a hump mold, sprayed with a thin layer of white slip, bisque fired to cone 02 and intentionally broken. Each shared was then glazed and fired differently. Only the lower right segment is raku fired. The upper left section was sawdust fired and the others were fired in electric and salt kilns prior to being reassembled with epoxy.

(1502–1555 A.D.) a disciple of Shuko, further developed Shuko's theories by introducing the concept of *wabi* which can be best described as the avoidance of luxury and falsity. Jo-o felt that human vanity must be absent from the tea ceremony. He relied on austere and simple analogies from nature to define this frame of mind.

Wabi

Sen-no Rikyu (1521–1591 A.D.), a disciple and student of Jo-o, perfected the philosophy of tea and carried it to its zenith. Rikyu is considered Japan's greatest Tea Master. As a close friend and retainer of Toyotomi Hideyoshi, the shogun, or supreme commander, of the army of

Japan, Rikyu reformed the rules of the tea ceremony completing its Japanization to suit the ordinary people and surroundings of Japan.

Wabi is the natural expression of feelings that are neither ostentatious nor imposing, and its spirit is the essence of the tea ceremony. A Buddhist might use the word *compassion* to describe the feeling of the ritual; an occidental might use the word *love*. It is that part of our being which emanates a simple and open love and an honest experience of union—whether it is the love of another human being or the empathy for leaves floating in the wind. The following is a selection of verses written by Rikyu explaining the meaning of *wabi* and the spirit of the tea ceremony:

Many though there be
Who with words or even hands
Know the Way of Tea.
Few there are or none at all,
Who can serve it from the heart.

If you have one pot
And can make your tea in it
That will do quite well.
How much does he lack himself
Who must have a lot of things.

When you hear the splash
Of the water drops that fall
Into the stone bowl
You will feel that all the dust
Of your mind is washed away.

In my little hut,
Whether people come or not
It is all the same.
In my heart there is no stir.
Of attraction or disgust.

There is no fixed rule
As to when the window should
Closed or open be.
It depends on how the moon
Or the snow their shadows cast.

Flowers of hill or dale
Put them in a simple vase
Full or brimming o'er.
But when you're arranging them
You must slip your heart in too.

Though invisible
There's a thing that should be swept
With our busy broom.
'Tis the dirt that ever clings
To the impure human heart.

Though you wipe your hands
And brush off the dust and dirt
From the tea vessels.
What's the use of all this fuss
If the heart is still impure?

When you take a sip
From the bowl of powder tea
There within it lies
Clear reflected in its depths
Blue of sky and gray of sea.

In the Dewy Path
And the tearoom's calm retreat
Host and guests have met.
Not an inharmonious note
Should disturb their quiet zest.

The rigid rules of the tea ceremony were to have a profound influence on Japanese art and the conduct of everyday life. The influence of the Tea Masters gave emphasis to the beauty of humility and the love of simplicity. Through their teachings, the spirit of the tea ceremony was to enter every aspect of Japanese life and culture. The popularity of the tea ceremony during the Momoyama period (1573–1614 A.D.) was responsible for the

Paul Soldner, unglazed and heavily smoked wheel-thrown pot, 12" high. The white slip decorations with iron and copper are glazed finger and palm prints.

appreciation and development of ceramics, particularly the ware used for the drinking of tea. Many types of ceremonial pottery were valued, each for its distinctive beauty, and each reflecting the Tea Master's philosophy and taste.

The Raku Family

If you study tea ware, you might encounter some of the following names:

Chien Yao or *Temmoku*, Sung Dynasty, 960–1127 A.D.

Raku, favored by Sen Rikyu, 1521–1591 A.D.

Asahi, one of the seven famous kilns of the tea master Kobori Enshu, 1579–1647 A.D.

Shino, Seto wares favored by the tea master Shino Soshin.

Oribe, wares made in Narumi for the tea master Furuta Oribe, 1544–1615 A.D.

Karatsu, Korean styled wares from the island of Kyushu, highly influenced by the Korean Yi Dynasty, 1392–1900 A.D.

There are many other names that could be included. These are listed simply to show that *Rakuyaki*—the raku object—was not the only kind of ware used in the tea ceremonies. Raku bowls, however, were favored by most connoisseurs. Besides being pleasing to the touch, and possessing that wonderful feeling of tranquility characteristic of *wabi*, the tea seemed to taste better in raku bowls. When the quality of water used for making tea was to be judged, or tested, the water was tasted from the raku tea bowl. Also, the highly grogged and porous clay body used for raku made an excellent insulated container for hot tea.

Also, raku ware was guided to fame in Kyoto by Sen Rikyu— because it was favored by him for use in the tea ceremony. The raku ware itself was originated by Chojiro, the son of a Korean tile maker. During the 1520's, Chojiro settled in Kyoto, after marrying into a Japanese family and becoming naturalized. Rikyu became so fond of Chojiro that he honored him by giving him his father's name of Tanaka. Each succeeding generation continued to use the name of Tanaka until the 1860's when Raku was taken as the family name.

Paul Soldner, altered wheel-thrown pot, 16" high. Partly glazed with iron and copper over a white slip. The white halo surrounding the iron and copper slip is a result of the clay reoxidizing along the edge of the slip during cooling.

The designs of Chojiro's soft earthenware reflected the wide bottom style of Korean tea bowls. His wares were usually glazed with one of two colors, and raku is still classified as either black or red raku ware. Chojiro's glazes were of the soft lead type, resembling those produced in the Chinese T'ang and Ming Dynasties.

The black glaze Chojiro developed is said to have two parts Kamogawa stone, mined from the Kamo River, to one part Japanese frit, made from ground lead glass. Kamogawa stone, or black stone, is similar in composition to barnard clay, with the same proportions of alumina, silica, and iron. Before glazing, the ware was bisqued to a bright cherry-red or orange at a temperature of about 1600° F. (If the bisque temperature were carried any higher the ware would become very vitreous and develop a harsh sounding ping when tapped by a fingernail or brushed as the tea was being stirred. The tea master, no doubt, would find such sounds disturbing to the serenity and peaceful atmosphere of the tea house.)

The red raku ware that is made in Japan today is said to be covered with a yellow-ochre slip prior to bisquing. Some red raku tea bowls have dark, smoky areas created by trapped carbon. These areas can be artificially induced by a special firing following the bisque firing. This is done by placing the ochre bowls in a box of burning charcoal and then dipping them in water to cool. Afterwards, a transparent lead glaze is applied by either brushing or dipping.

It is not known if a similar formula was used by Chojiro. He might have used a lead and Japanese frit glaze over a reddish clay body, or he may have used a glaze containing red iron oxide and even twice as much ochre. Reds are difficult to achieve and they are usually made in a muffle (a protective fireclay box within the kiln) and fired at temperatures well below the 1600° F. usually used for bisquing or the higher glaze temperatures used for black raku. It should also be noted that the red raku ware was often allowed to cool slowly and naturally in the kiln. Chojiro probably glaze-fired his raku ware in a wood-burning muffle kiln, and watched the firing through a hole in the lid. The correct temperature was determined by the color of the ware and the kiln's interior, or by the removal of glazed draw rings. At the correct temperature the ware—especially if it were glazed black—would be removed from the hot kiln with long-handled tongs, and immersed in a concentrated solution of green tea. Not all ware is quenched in a tea solution; some ware is removed from the kiln and placed directly on cool bricks or tiles and allowed to oxidize. But, the soft and subtle crackling or crazing of the glaze can best be achieved by allowing the ware to oxidize a few seconds before it is quenched.

Among the tea bowls that Chojiro made, seven became very famous:

One of Chojiro's bowls is called *Daikoku*, The Great Black. It is a little over three inches high and no more than four inches in diameter. It was admired for its rustic and quiet appearance, and was one of Rikyu's most cherished possessions.

Another, called *Toyobo*, was given to the Toyobo Hall at the Shinnyodo Temple by Rikyu. Both bowls are owned by the Konoike family of Osaka and are considered to be in accord with the spirit of *wabi*.

Two more of the famous seven are named *Kengyo* and *Kimamori*, because they were not appreciated by the connoisseurs. Once, when Rikyu went to Chojiro for tea bowls, the potter had only one. He told Rikyu that the reason he had that one bowl was that, like the blind minstrel, no one wanted it; that bowl was named *Kengyo*. *Kimamori* is the name given to the last piece of fruit left on a tree as a "guard" during the winter. Rikyu asked his pupils to select the bowls they liked best. One of the ten bowls that he showed them was not chosen by any of the pupils. Rikyu purposely called it *Kimamori*.

The fifth bowl was named *Hayabune*, meaning swift ship, because Rikyu had a swift ship sent from Kyoto to Korea to bring the bowl for use in serving tea.

The sixth bowl Rikyu named *Rinzai*, because it possessed the preeminence of the great Zen monk *Rinzai*.

The last of Chojiro's seven famous bowls is called the *Hachibiraki*, the Inauguration bowl, because Rikyu had planned to use it for the first time in serving tea to a powerful shogun.

The name raku comes from a gold seal granted to Chojiro's young apprentice, Jokei, by the shogun Hideyoshi. Until that time, the ware was called "now ware" or "Kyoto ware." It was six years after Chojiro's death when the honor was bestowed. The gold seal was given in memory of Chojiro and bore the ideograph *raku*, a symbol that, freely translated, means enjoyment, contentment, pleasure, and happiness. The written character for the word raku comes from Hideyoshi's pleasure pavilion in Kyoto named Ju-raku-tei; Chojiro and his workshop had made roof tiles for this pavilion.

Following is a list of the generations of the house of Raku:

THIRD GENERATION:	Donyu, the son of Jokei. Died 1656.
FOURTH GENERATION:	Ichinyu, the son of Donyu. Died 1696.
FIFTH GENERATION:	Sonyu, a pupil of Ichinyu. Died 1716.
SIXTH GENERATION:	Sanyu, the adopted son of Sonyu. Died 1739.
SEVENTH GENERATION:	Chonyu, Sanyu's younger brother. Died 1770.
EIGHTH GENERATION:	Tokunyu, Chonyu's adopted son. Died 1774.
NINTH GENERATION:	Ryonyu, Tokunyu's son. Died 1834.
TENTH GENERATION:	Tannyu, the son of Ryonyu. Died 1854.
ELEVENTH GENERATION:	Keinyu, Tannyu's son. Died 1902.
TWELFTH GENERATION:	Konyu (1857–1932).
THIRTEENTH GENERATION:	Seinyu (1885–1944).
FOURTEENTH GENERATION:	Kakunyu (1918–1980).
FIFTEENTH GENERATION:	Kichizaemon (1949–).

Tea Masters and Potters

Ogata Kenzan (1661–1742 A.D.) was one of Japan's greatest potters and also one of the world's great artists. Besides being acclaimed for his painting and poetry, he was a famous Tea Master. This title and honor was granted only to a true artist who had sufficient awareness and insight into nature and man. There were other famous potters who were also tea masters, but many potters were overshadowed by the Tea Masters for whom they made tea bowls. Although Chojiro was the potter who originated the ware, it is often—even now—referred to as "Rikyu ware," not because it was made by Rikyu, but because Rikyu was Japan's most famous Tea Master and raku ware was prized and made famous by him.

Little would be known of raku pottery in today's Western world had it not been for Bernard Leach. Leach, an Englishman, studied pottery in Japan with a sixth generation representative of Ogata Kenzan. Between 1911 and 1920, with the exceptions of the years 1915 through 1917 which he spent in China, Leach made raku pottery in Tokyo. He became a seventh generation representative of the Kenzan tradition, with certification from his master, and continued to produce raku pottery in England between 1920 and 1930. His book, *A Potter's Book,* published in 1940, is credited with introducing and describing raku pottery outside of Japan.

Warren Gilbertson is probably the first American to introduce raku ware to this country. After Gilbertson returned from Japan, he exhibited over 250 pieces of pottery at the Art Institute of Chicago. It was during this exhibit, in November and December of 1941, that a number of raku pieces were shown. The simple techniques used in raku attracted some American potters in the early 1950's, but raku was not pursued seriously in the United States until the 1960s.

Paul Soldner is most responsible for the direction and popularity of raku in this country. In 1960 Soldner started making post fired reduction raku pottery in Los Angeles, California. Many of his pieces are wheel-thrown bulbous forms that have been altered by the addition of clay and other surface treatments. They often reflect an illusive, subtle, yet vigorous beauty. Soldner's works and those of many other contemporaries somehow manage to perpetuate the fundamental and universal rhythms of life associated with raku pottery.

Whether or not today's raku potters should reflect the philosophical Oriental heritage in their ceramic forms is a matter of personal choice. If an American potter were to incorporate some other standard of form for expression, as seen in the work represented in this book, there would be no need to feel any apprehension; it is not the form or even the philosophy of raku that is important—the form will disappear in time, it is sure to be broken—it is the experience that lives and moves life forward.

Michael Gwinup, wheel thrown plate made with a Kyanite clay body and an expressive energy that celebrates life, 20" in diameter.

2
The Ceremony of Tea,
Cha-No-Yu

The Tea Ceremony, like raku, is almost synonomous with Japan. For centuries the tea ceremony, called *Cha-No-Yu* (hot water for tea), has been responsible for creating an appreciation and understanding of raku pottery. The tea ceremony used raku tea bowls because they symbolized the beauty, the simple and unassuming qualities, that were in harmony with everyday life.

The Japanese use the word *Shibui* to express this quality of beauty: a beauty that might be associated with the fine aging of old bronze, virtue and unassuming tastefulness. Because of its manifold relationships with philosophy and religion and its emphasis on simplicity and natural beauty, a knowledge of the tea ceremony is helpful in understanding and appreciating its influence both in the field of ceramics and on the conduct of life. Understanding this quality of beauty sets the mood for the making of raku pottery much in the same way a tea garden is used to set the mood for the tea ceremony.

Though the ceremony itself contains a mixture of the ancient cultures of India and China, it was the Japanese spirit that transformed and adapted the ceremony into the epitome of Japanese institutions and civilization. The ceremony derives its origin from Chinese Zen Buddhism and the elaborate ritual of drinking tea before the image of Bodhidharma, the

Raku Tea Bowl bearing the mark of Jokei.

semi-legendary figure of the first patriarch of Chinese Zen. Perhaps the greatest contribution made by Zen to the secularization of the Japanese ceremony of tea was the concept of equal importance: the littleness of greatness and the greatness of littleness in all things. The whole ideal behind the ceremonial form of tea drinking is the Zen concept of no distinction of importance between incidents of life.

There are almost as many approaches to the tea ceremony as there are tea masters, but they differ little in the essentials. There are three distinct phases in the full tea gathering: a meal called *Kaiseki* is the first phase; the second, followed by a brief rest in the garden, is *Koicha* or the thick-tea phase; and the third, the thin-tea phase, is known as *Usucha*. Any one, or all three phases, may be chosen and served by the host.

The *Usucha* phase is the most popular and usually the only one served because it takes three or four hours (which includes recesses spent in the garden) in order to properly serve all three. The ceremony in its entirety is usually reserved for special occasions, such as the celebration of a birth, or those special occasions or holidays for which a Westerner might give a dinner party.

To insure an atmosphere of quiet serenity and isolation from worldly distractions, an elaborate code of etiquette and rules govern the ritual and the conduct of the participants. These rules demand strict observance. The practices, many of which were instituted by Rikyu, begin with

the host extending the invitation days in advance to not more than five, but not less than three, guests. Frequently, there is a guest of honor or number one guest, for whom the ceremony is given. The day before the ceremony the guests call on the host to express their thanks in advance. The day of the ceremony the host is busy with elaborate preparations: cleaning the tearoom, privy, and garden; selecting the utensils and alcove decoration; and planning the food.

The Day of the Ceremony

The guests arrive early to change footwear and, perhaps, some clothing. They assemble in the outer garden which also contains the waiting arbor and the privy. Here they are to admire the garden and, in effect, shed their worldly cares. If no guest of honor has been chosen by the host, the guests will now decide who will be "guest number one": the guest whose lead the others will follow in a predetermined manner from the outer garden through the middle gate and into the inner garden.

When the host is ready the guests are summoned to the tearoom by way of the garden path connecting the teahouse and the arbor. The walk on the path is intended to remove the thought and spirit of the outside world and to produce a quiet and tranquil mood that will be conducive to the serenity of the tearoom. The intended sensation of the walk varies. Some tea masters aim at purity of spirit, others seek solitude, while some—like Rikyu—sought to achieve loneliness. The ingenuity involved in the planning and preparation of the garden has much to do with a particular effect. Stepping stones, chosen for their irregularity are arranged with scrupulous care; a quiet rock-lined pond might be placed where it will reflect an autumn moon; an earthen bridge could pass fragrant pines and lead to a hill of maple trees containing a moss-covered stone lantern. Although the garden path would have been cleaned only hours before the ceremony, the host will often take great pains to produce an effect of the rustic naturalness by the careful placement of dried pine needles or

A totally serene view of the pathway approaching a teahouse in Kyoto. Note the stone washbasin in the center foreground.

Japanese teahouse and garden at Sambo-in (near Kyoto) used by Hideyoshi.

by the careful shaking of a tree limb so that the loosened leaves might add their natural beauty to the path. As they silently approach the teahouse, the guests pause just outside the tearoom at a special stone washbasin filled with peaceful sounding trickles of running water. With a dipper, they perform a formal purification of the rinsing of the hands and mouth, and then pass directly into the tearoom.

The opening to the tearoom through which they pass is quite small. It is a standard twenty-seven inches by thirty-six inches, a size originally decided by Rikyu, causing each guest to enter by bending in a manner symbolic of humility. One by one the guests noiselessly pass from the vexations of the world outside and enter, in an order of precedence formerly agreed upon, into the sanctuary of the tearoom. Prior to seating, the guests stop to admire the painted calligraphy on a scroll in the alcove, which is derived from the altar in Zen chapels, and perhaps the tiny incense holder and the raku or porcelain water jar.

Robert Piepenburg, sculptural forms, 23", 21" and 22" high.

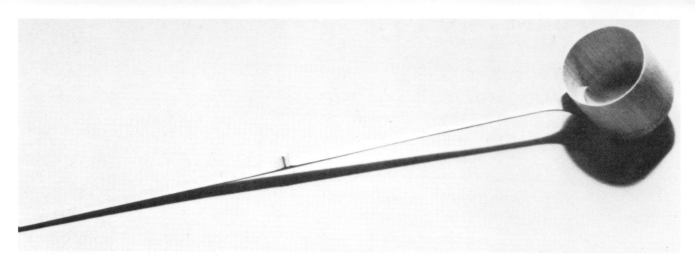

Bamboo water dipper, 16¼" long.

When the guests are silently seated and there is no sound but the bubbling of water boiling in the iron kettle, which is heated by a seventeen-inch-square sunken fire box called the *Ro*, the host will make his appearance. In the summer, or when there is no hearth, a three-footed furnace is used and a trivet is placed in the inside bottom to support the kettle.

The host does not enter from the guest doorway but through another entrance adjoining a preparation area where the utensils are cleaned and arranged. After bowing and greeting his guests, the host sits with his body at a forty-five-degree angle to the hearth, facing his guest of honor with whom he will speak.

In a short time the host will serve the *Kaiseki*, a simple but excellent meal, that has been prepared with the utmost care. The meal might consist of no more than soup and cakes, or it might include pickles, broiled fish, roasted chestnuts, vegetables, mushrooms, and seaweed. It is not customary for the host to eat with his guests.

At times during the meal, there is the drinking of sake followed by the serving of sweets. Then there is the ceremonial cleaning of the chopsticks and the mouth with salt or herb-flavored warm water. The guests will then take a recess in the garden, to chat and await the sounding of the gong to signal their return to the tearoom, and the ritual serving of tea.

Serving the Tea

Upon their return to the tearoom, the guests may find the scroll in the alcove replaced with a simple flower arrangement. After the prescribed acts of etiquette have been completed the *Koicha*, or thick-tea, is ready to be served. It is prepared from leaves of the highest quality that have been especially harvested and processed for the tea rites. If there are five guests, up to sixteen scoops of the powdered tea are removed from the thick-tea caddy and put into a tea bowl. The bowl may or may not be raku, depending upon the personal taste of the host, or the school of tea with which he is associated. A special spoon is used for transferring the powdered tea; it is usually hand-carved bamboo, and made by a tea master or philosopher. Hot water, taken from the kettle with a bamboo dipper, is poured into the bowl and the tea beaten with a bamboo whisk. (Thin tea forms a frothy soup resembling "liquid jade," thick tea does not.) The whisk, split into threads at one end and conforming to the bottom contour of the bowl, makes a soft, rushing sound, far more pleasing than the sound made by a metal implement.

In turn, each guest drinks a portion of the tea. After raising the bowl in a gesture of thanks they will take one sip, compliment the host on its flavor, noisily take two or three more sips, and then pass the bowl on until each guest has tasted the tea. Protocol demands that each guest wipe the part of the bowl touched by his lips with a small white cloth before pass-

The guest of honor goes first to the alcove to admire the painting and flower arrangement.

Christy A. Bartlett, Director of the Urasenke Foundation of San Francisco, wisks tea in a bowl or chawan.

ing it. When the bowl has been emptied of tea the guest of honor may ask that the bowl be passed again to allow for closer inspection and appreciation of its qualities. The spoon and tea caddy may also be circulated for appreciation. A small silk square is often used by the guests when handling the tea utensils. This ends the second phase of the ceremony.

Although two or three hours have passed since the ceremony began, the guests are neither bored nor tired, as they were most carefully selected by the host for their congeniality. The third or final phase is marked by the serving of the thin tea. The thin tea, served at this less formal yet most often used sitting, is slightly more bitter than the thick tea. The tea is removed from the thin-tea caddy, and prepared in a similar manner. The general difference is that each guest empties the tea bowl, wipes the rim with his fingers, wipes his fingers with a small white paper, and then returns the bowl directly to the host. The host washes it out with hot water, empties the water in the waste-water holder, wipes it with a small linen cloth, and whisks new tea in the bowl for the next guest. The bowl is then presented best side forward to the guest. The guest, with careful and precise movements, turns it in his hands so that he does not sip from the best side. A sweet jelly confection is also served at this time.

With departing saluations the guests take their leave. They return, as etiquette demands, on the following day to convey their appreciation and thanks for the host's kindness.

Teaism

Japanese civilization might be referred to as a tea civilization. By Western standards, the tea ceremony is not religious but rather a social institution. Its manifestations might be better understood if the tea rites are compared to some of the practices of Western religions; the similarities are many. Parishioners arrive at the church (tearoom) before the service (ceremony), sit quietly (meditate), and wait for the entrance of the priest (host). The altar (alcove) will display a symbolic cloth covering (scroll) and perhaps an arrangement of flowers. The priest (host) upon entering will symbolically greet his congregation (guests). In many churches Holy Communion will be the climax of the service (ceremony)

Raku tea bowl, middle Edo period.

Bamboo tea wisk (4¼" high) and spoon (7¼" long). The tea bowl is an early work of Rev. N. S. Kobori (Daitokuji, Kyoto, Japan) and is owned by Sandor B. Brent.

with the serving and receiving of the bread (confection) and the wine (tea). Other parallels exist in the way the sections of the ceremony are cherished by the participants.

Religious artifacts are often exceedingly ornate and frequently valued as much for their luxurious appearance as for their religious antiquity and association. I have heard of some raku tea bowls belonging to great tea masters valued at over $100,000 because of the personal association. However, raku tea bowls, in addition to their associative value, are adored for their simple naturalness and avoidance of luxury.

The architecture and interiors of churches and the architecture and interiors of teahouses are also fundamentally similar in purpose; they are both designed and consecrated for a specific ceremony.

Early tearooms, and many modern ones, are simply areas in the home partitioned off from other areas with screens. The tearoom, whether it is part of the house or a separate teahouse, is used only for ceremonial purposes. The proportions of the room vary. In Japan the woven mats called *tatami* are an architectural standard of measurement— *tatami* are three feet by six feet by one-and-one-half-inch thick rough straw mats with a finely woven straw cover. Tea ceremony rooms are usually anywhere from two to four and one-half mats in area. The popular size is four and one-half mats.

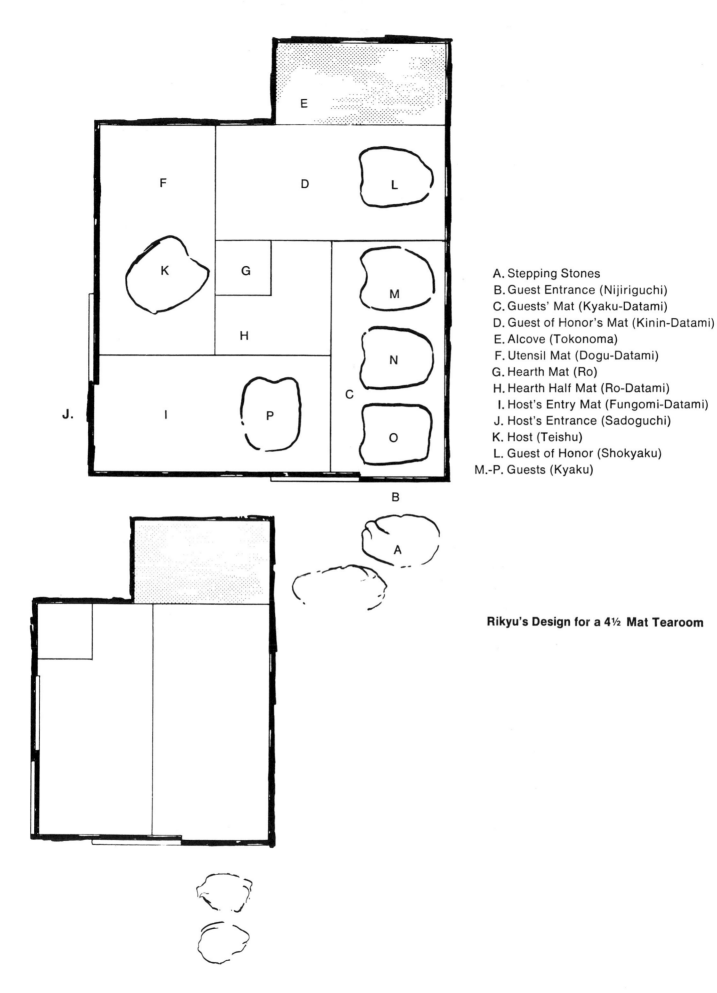

A. Stepping Stones
B. Guest Entrance (Nijiriguchi)
C. Guests' Mat (Kyaku-Datami)
D. Guest of Honor's Mat (Kinin-Datami)
E. Alcove (Tokonoma)
F. Utensil Mat (Dogu-Datami)
G. Hearth Mat (Ro)
H. Hearth Half Mat (Ro-Datami)
I. Host's Entry Mat (Fungomi-Datami)
J. Host's Entrance (Sadoguchi)
K. Host (Teishu)
L. Guest of Honor (Shokyaku)
M.-P. Guests (Kyaku)

Rikyu's Design for a 4½ Mat Tearoom

Rikyu's Design for a 2 Mat Tearoom

Top, *Sister Celeste Mary Bourke, raku altar and appointments in a small chapel at Siena Heights College. The three supporting boxes and altar top are smoked clay only. Bottom, The candle holders, cruets, chalices, and tabernacle, which opens at the top, are covered with a transparent glaze.*

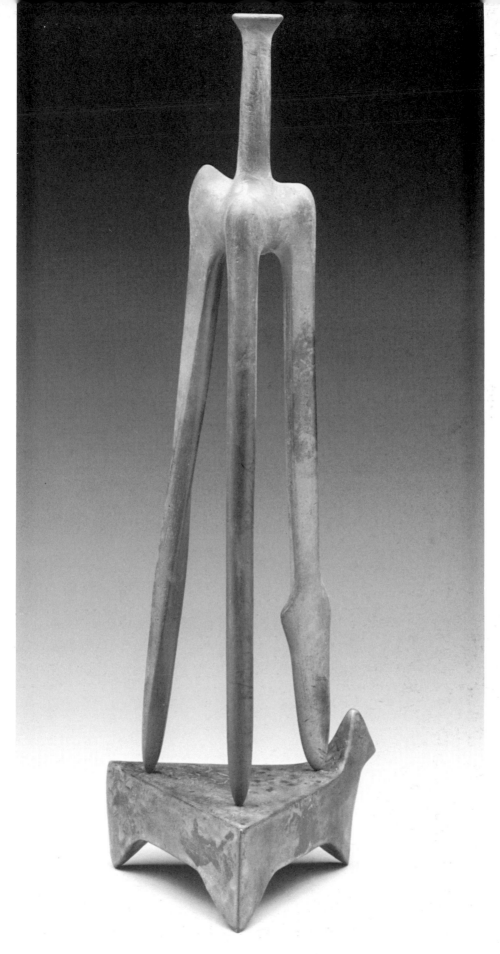

Richard Hirsch, Vessel and Stand #28, 25".

Ben Pearlman, handbuilt bowl formed by pressing together thick slads of clay inside of a plaster drape mold. The unglazed organic edges provide a natural yet dramatic contrasts to the smoothness of the interior surface obtained from the use of both metal and rubber ribs. Prior to glazing, several thin layers of slip, made from a slaked-down porcelain clay body, were brushed onto the area to be glazed. The slip functions as a primer, allowing for a whiter glaze finish, 4" x 18" x 22".

Teahouses built in the traditional style reflect a deliberate form of architectural purity that is unprepossessing. Although they resemble nothing more than a straw-covered hut with mud-covered walls, they are made from the finest materials and with meticulous care, and often cost as much as the main house. The secret of the tearoom lies in its undecorated walls and its simple unadorned beauty. There are no distractions. The room is calm, and its ambience does not distract the mind, but rather, frees the participant to become aware of and recognize the beauty of other things. It is often said that the tearoom draws out the beauty of the utensils.

Architecturally Rikyu revolutionized tearoom design. Using the standard four-and-one-half-mat floor plan established by Jo-o, Rikyu did away with Jo-o's open veranda design which made the garden and room's interior a single space. With the exception of a few small windows, the tearoom was to become a cosmos in itself—independent in architectural style and independent of the outside world. Searching for structural purity Rikyu substituted natural log posts for the planed and square supports. Ornaments and decorated door panels were eliminated, and the walls were made of clay similar to the clay used for the walls of simple farmhouses.

Rikyu did not recognize social rank in the tearoom and insisted that men of different status forget their distinctions and aim for spiritual accord. To encourage deeper spiritual accord, Rikyu reduced the floor area from four and one-half tatami mats (the minimum space necessary to prevent an

Rick Foris, Tea Pot with Pedestal, glazed, raku fired, smoked and painted with acrylics, 10" x 12" x 15".

aristocrat from bumping knees with someone of lesser station) to two mats. It was such disregard for rank and station that angered Rikyu's fierce patron, Hideyoshi, who eventually condemned Rikyu to die, with honor, by Rikyu's own hand.

Tearooms and the tea ceremony, like Japan itself, have undergone many changes since the time of Rikyu and Chojiro. Traditionally, tea encompassed the culture and all the art forms that are Japan. To ask to what extent a role it plays in Japanese art and life today is to ask what it exemplifies to each individual. To some it might mean little compared to the universal trends and intrusions that accompany expanding technologies. It is, however, improbable for the spirit of tea not to exist somewhere within, hopefully seeking expression. The spirit of tea is like the spirit of life. To ask contemporary raku potters to concern themselves with it might be too much, yet it lingers deep in the nativity of raku pottery. To envision its latent potential to affect our work and lives, one must come face to face with its meaning. To understand the spirit of tea is to delve into the mystery of ourselves and the metamorphosis implicit in clay.

Be prepared for the moment
For we were once a moment
Becoming a moment
To become a moment
To become a moment
To become
To be.

RON ALDRICH

———————

I embrace this man of clay with holiness
This man, who sows the seed, the holy clay
From which the seeds of life are growing
Earth of hope and nourishment
Perpetually erupting in forms of love.
Deeply, he is the
Earth of first beginnings, of all the aging times
The fired masterpiece of all these burning cosmos.

JUDY PIEPENBURG

Gallery

Ana England, Multiply, fabracted from hollowed out slabs of various thicknesses. Fired in sections and glued onto plywood with PC-7 epoxy.

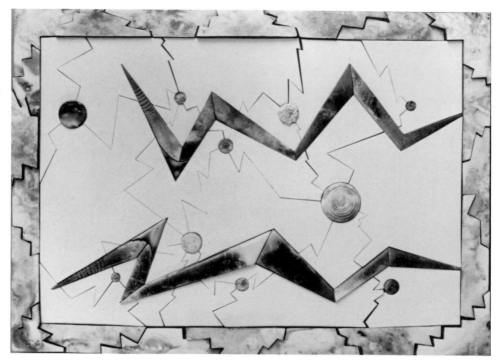

*Ana England, New Wave
Particle Dancing: Due,
2³/₄″ × 32¹/₂″ × 45″.*

Paul Soldner, #897, 8″ × 28″ × 47″.

Monti Mayrend, wall piece made from broken slabs assembled from the back side, 12" × 12".

Chou, Pang-Ling, Reciprocal Treaty of Simple Affection, clay combined with recycled castoffs is innovatively used in the "Teapot Mutants" series to combine the past with the contemporary, 5" × 12" × 13".

Dianne Logan, clay slabs with found rusted metal, 9″ × 6″ and 5″ × 5″.

Kae L. Clement, 5 Dolphins, 5¹/₂″ × 8¹/₂″ × 21″.

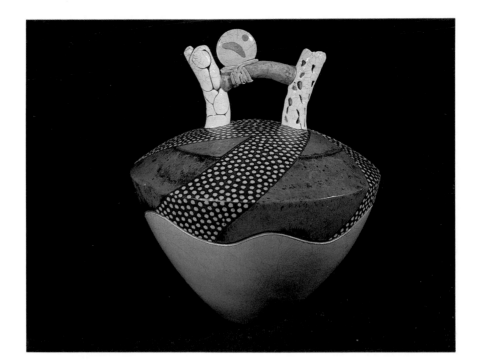

Kurt Weiser, form with lid, 12½" × 12½" × 15".

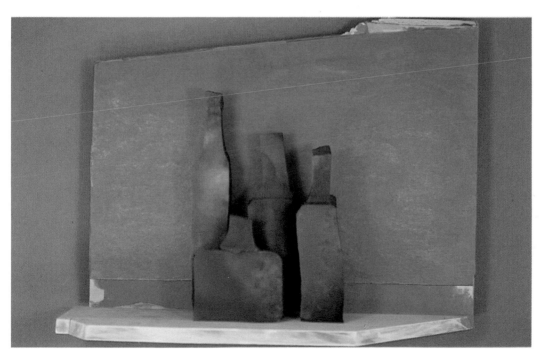

Nancy Selvin, Modest Morandian Construction, slip cast clay and mixed media, 36" × 26" × 6½".

Gail Piepenburg, Diptych, slab built wall piece with some commercial glaze, 2" × 22" × 34".

Jim Leedy, Expressionistic Plate, hand built raku with resin glaze, 5" × 16" × 17".

Jim Connell, Carved Teapot, 13" × 16".

Penelope Fleming, Baffin Isle Triptych, 36″ × 54″ × 5″.

Susan and Steven Kemenyffy, Waiting for Japan, raku diptych approx. 30″ × 48″.

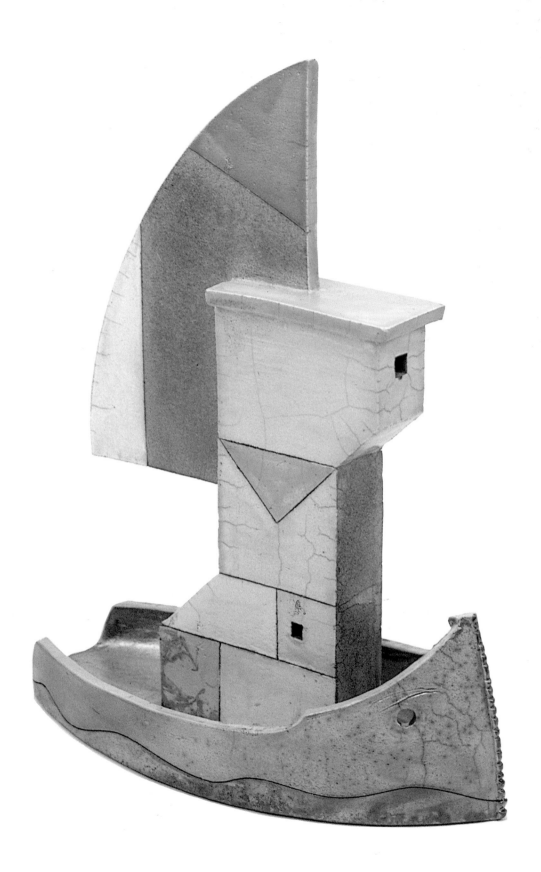

Peter Kuentzel, Alicia, from his Miami boat series, 7″ × 14″ × 17″.

Chou, Pang-Ling, It Is Enough to Make a Day have Glory, clay and found objects, 5″ × 13″ × 14″.

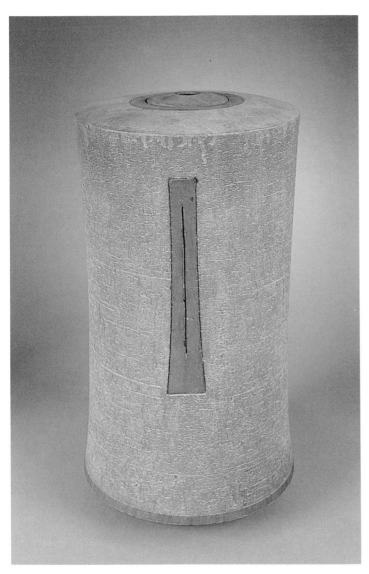

Steve Olszewski, thrown vessel with lid and painted sur-
face, 9" × 20".

Robert Piepenburg, Standing Within
Motion, clay parts assembled wet with one
inch lengths of stainless steel rod, 23"
high.

James Lawton, Teapot with Tray, 12" × 17".

Steve Wieneke, Sunrise, 4" × 11" × 7".

Chris Thompson, Balanced Bowl, 26" in diameter.

Rafael A. Duran, Vessel #16, 13" × 11" × 10½".

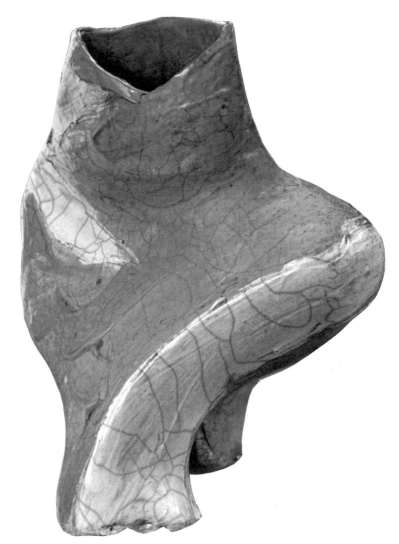

Wayne Higby, Towerlands Winter, five landscape containers with lids, 8¹/₂" × 15" × 34³/₄", (collection of Roger Robinson).

3

Clay: Material and Medium

Raku pottery is earth derived. Clay has little value in itself; any value it may have is based upon man and his relationship to the clay.

The raku tea bowl is more than a receptacle for tea; it carries human sensory experience. Clay is more than a material, it is a medium for unlimited form and expression. It can, without the use of any tool—except the miracle of man's hands—be made to bear forth, incarnate, our sense of life. As reasoning beings we are sometimes aware of the unity between clay and man; but when we function as potters, we often become completely involved in production and the technical process of the work— sometimes to the exclusion of everything else. Although in this chapter we will discuss clay in the material-technical sense, a potter should always remember that potting—like life—is not a technical process. A few potters approach clay as a scientific exercise, but most learn about and become involved with the technical aspects only when this knowledge is needed.

David Hines attaching a leather hard clay addition to one of his tall forms built around a cardboard cylinder. Later it will be finished with a variety of glazes including commercial underglazes.

To make good pottery there must be a feeling for clay. Become involved with your material, get to know as much as you can about clay—the chemical make-up, the mechanics of processing the clay, the techniques for forming pieces, etc.—but never become so technically oriented that you are disloyal to your senses and feelings for the clay as a medium for expression and as a material in itself.

Encountering the Medium

It is difficult to discuss pottery without including the invisible life spirit brought to the work by the potter—his or her mind, imagination, emotions, and very being. This spirit can be related to the spirit of the clay. Before telling my beginning students about the methods and procedures for forming clay, I usually conduct them through an "encounter session" with the substance itself.

As a group I invite them to dig a lump of clay from the barrel using their fingers and become acquainted with the substance by working and playing with it. In summer sessions we start by mixing the clay outdoors.

The students, in bare feet, form a tight circle. With the help of a hose and a hoe, powdered clay is trampled from a dry to a liquid to a plastic material. After the students become familiar with this initial tactile experience, more directed activities are attempted. The clay is rolled, pinched, dropped on the table, thrown on the table, pressed, twisted, tasted (chewed, not swallowed), poked, smoothed, and silently, with closed eyes, fondled. Some of the unending possibilities are explored.

Immediately following this exploratory and tactile phase, I usually ask the students to react to the clay as an artistic and creative medium. They are asked to work with the clay in the most imaginative way they can. Some students experiment with textures made by their own fingers, some use objects that are found in the studio. Another request might take them outside the studio with a lump of clay to find and bring back impressions of textures found in nature.

Next they create a rigid, structured, geometric type of form—with neat, sharp corners, made by pounding the clay on a table. They also

Sean Najjar painting colored slips on a series of leather-hard forms made from thrown and extruded parts.

experiment with free-flowing organic forms by sliding the clay on the table as it is thrown. Sometimes we break up into groups of three or four and go off for fifteen minutes and make, completely through nonverbal communication, a community form. Other times the students isolate themselves for about ten minutes and create specific shapes or objects, such as a cylindrical piece so that they can experience the uniqueness of individual expression within the confines of an assigned form.

Each group of students has its own personality and, in a sense, it is this group composition that determines the direction and tempo that will be taken. It is essential that an open and running dialogue about the actions and reactions of each student is maintained. This communication helps to reveal ways in which one is prevented from feeling and experiencing the clay fully and honestly.

Each student's work is always discussed by everyone in the class before destruction—yes, destruction. One at a time the students destroy their forms and shapes, not because death is needed to bring new life, but because of the self-awareness this act inspires. Students will often slowly

Wedging clay. This is that shared moment when clay and potter meet and touch each other for the first time . . . evoking an unspoken and mysterious dialogue that ultimately unites and directs both.

Student encounter with clay. Although clay appears simple, it is limitless. Like ourselves, there are no formulas for understanding clay and working with it. The encounter is directed toward knowing, appreciating, understanding, accepting, and, most of all, letting things be what they are.

squeeze the clay between their fingers, or quietly fold the clay down on the table with the palm of their hand, they do not simply throw the clay down, as might be expected. Some students, who had wrinkled their noses as if to say "what an ugly material," when they first took the clay from the barrel, might be almost in tears when it is their turn to demolish their creation.

As a teacher of pottery, I am always trying to make the student the subject of my course—to make each student aware of themselves. The "encounter with clay," that I have described, is part of the self-analysis and introspection that I believe leads to true expression. The ultimate goal is to make the material and the expression of the person, through the material, become as one. When this happens, the artist-craftsman recognizes the power and potential of the clay as a unique and universal medium and of themselves as a unique creature within the universality of humankind.

A small group of students new to clay working together—nonverbally—to make a community form: a phase of the encounter that arouses conscious-ness, participation, excitement, experiences of meaning and eventually . . .

The Clay

Clay for use in raku can be found almost anywhere. The only requirements are that the clay must mature chemically at or above 1600° F, contain enough coarse or refractory filler material—such as grog, sand, kyanite, molocite, talc, etc.—to withstand the thermal shock, respond well to the technique of forming, and successfully survive the firing.

Clay can be used directly from the ground with no further processing. You can often find very usable clay by yourself; start your prospecting on surface outcroppings. If you want to dig and use native clays you might get some assistance in locating natural clay deposits by asking your state geologist.

Clay is basically decomposed rock. It is made by the wearing away of rocks for millions of years. Temperature, wind, water, ice, and natural plants have also served a part in the formation of clay. Look near riverbeds, dried creek beds, eroded hillsides, or any place that digging or

Clay may be found near creek beds or as surface outcroppings of the landscape.

Clay being unloaded from the mixer. For raku, the openness of clay made in a dough mixer is preferred to the dense clay from a pug mill.

excavations have taken place. The quality of the clay you find can be recognized by studying the "crack patterns."

If there are deep cracks and many clear patterns are imprinted in the clay, and the clay is very "plastic," then it is probably quite pure, and not suitable for raku because it isn't porous enough. This clay might require the addition of grog or sand to increase the ability to withstand the shock of the raku firing technique and the use of tongs. If the patterns and cracks in the clay are not strongly pronounced the deposit is probably contaminated with sand or organic matter which should make it suitable for raku. If a clay source should prove to be too plastic or non-porous to survive the firing without cracking, one might add a refractory material such as sand. Experimentation might be started by firing clay containing various amounts of sand.

The processing of clay dug from a local deposit requires that it be dried and broken into small chunks prior to slaking—soaking in water till it crumbles. When it breaks up into a slip consistency, it needs only to be mixed and poured through a screen to remove any remaining lumps or stones, and placed on a plaster of paris slab to remove the excess moisture from the clay.

The making of a workable raku clay body by blending various purchased materials is a simple procedure. A satisfactory body should contain as its main ingredient a high temperature fire clay, or bounding clay, that matures beyond 1800° F. These can be purchased from most local refractory companies and if large quantities are ordered there is quite a savings. The other basic ingredient needed is a filler. In the ratio of 10 to 30 percent fillers allow clay bodies to survive the thermal shock of raku firing and reduction without helplessly cracking. Grog, the best known filler, is a refractory clay that has been fired and ground into granules. The 20–28 mesh works well. Grog is often referred to as the bones of the clay because it adds structure and lessens shrinkage during drying and thermal shock during firing. It, too, is found at most local refractory companies. Washed silica sand and beach sand in the 25–50 mesh range are excellent alternatives to grog. Not only are they half as expensive, but they adhere to the clay better. In addition, sand, unlike grog, is absorbent and clings to clay which makes it possible to create larger shapes; and when firing at the temperature necessary for raku, there is no noticeable swelling or protruding of silica sand from the surface of the fired clay like there is with stoneware. Kyanite, a highly refractory alumina-silica ore, is, in my opinion, the most beneficial filler to have in a raku clay body . . . especially if you are hand building large or exceptionally

Kegham Tazian, Architectural Fragments, 6" × 7" × 10".

thick pieces. Steven Kemenyffy is credited with discovering the strong magic that this particular ingredient can bring to raku clay. He and his wife, Susan, have consistently been able to transcend the technical menace of thermal breakage in their large sculptures and wall pieces with the added dimensions of kyanite to their clay formula. Mullite, a calcinated form of kyanite, can also be used as a clay body filler. Although it is non-plastic, it does strengthen the clay and reduce thermal stress. In the fifty percent range, it is often used to make kiln shelves and posts. Molochite, a 22 mesh porcelain grog, is another good filler as is sawdust. For a long while, I was adding twenty percent sawdust, that had first been screened through a large mesh sieve, to my handbuilding and throwing bodies. The amazing occurrence with this material was not that it made the pieces so much lighter after bisque firing, but rather that it seemed to age the clay and render it plastic almost over night. Some other non-clay, heat shock and crack resistent additives that can be used in various combinations include: walnut shells, coarse wollastonite, vermiculite, zonolite, pearlite and talc.

When fire clay, filler and water are mixed in the correct proportions, a very satisfactory raku clay body should be the result, especially if the clay is wedged and stored for several days before it is used. The formula for my hand-building raku body, by volume, is as follows:

1	Cedar Heights Fireclay* (50 mesh)
1	Hawthorn Bonding Fireclay* (35 mesh)
3/4	Virginia Kyanite (35 mesh)
1/4	Lake Michigan beach sand (45 mesh) optional

*These two Missouri fireclays are fairly clean and plastic . . . and so far have not contributed to surface calcium/lime popouts.

Jordan clay can be added to make the body more workable and the clay would then act as a plastic low-grade fire clay but, unfortunately, it is no longer available. Ball clay, a very plastic secondary clay, can be substituted for Jordon at the expense of high shrinkage (fifteen percent at maturity) if good plasticity is wanted. Bentonite, a volcanic clay, can also be added (do not exceed two percent) to make the clay more plastic. I have stopped using it because it is difficult to distribute through the body. It must be slaked in water before using, and hardly seems worth the effort. For a more plastic raku body that is suitable for work on the wheel, I use the following formula by volume:

2	Cedar Heights Goldart
1	Tennessee Ball Clay
1/4	Virginia Kyanite (48 mesh)

Jerry L. Caplan, Young Girl, 12" diameter form with reduction stenciled image. The image is scratched through a finely sieved clay slip (made from the clay body itself) applied to the bisque surface. The dried slip/ stencil is removed after firing and smoke reduction to reveal the carbonized design.

Kari Rasmussen, thrown forms, cut/broken and completed from the fragments of their initial shape, top piece: 10" tall, bottom piece: 8" tall.

You might think that clay of a finer mesh, such as a 200 mesh air-floated fire clay, would increase plasticity, but if the 50 mesh clay is added to water and thoroughly mixed, you will be unable to tell the difference. Fire clay, regardless of its mesh, slakes down uniformly in solution. The 50 mesh, in addition to being less expensive than the smaller sized 200 mesh, is less hazardous because there is less chance of inhaling the dust and less is given off during handling and mixing. Plasticity is also increased by aging or storing the mixed clay in an airtight plastic bag or crock. Colloidal conditions that evolve through bacterial growth improve the clay's plasticity. The longer the clay is aged the better, but improvements are noticeable in two to five days.

White Raku Body (Joe Zajac)		**Throwing Raku Body (David Powell)**	
50%	Kaolin - #6 Tile Clay	40%	Fireclay
10%	Fireclay - A.P. Green	23%	Talc
10%	Ball Clay - Kentucky OM 4	18%	Kyanite
15%	Silica Sand	10%	Ball Clay
10%	Mullite	9%	Mullite
5%	Wollastonite	1%	Red Iron Oxide

David Hines, Twilight Flight, an aesthetically playful expression of spiritual wholeness and creativity seemingly enriched by that magic supportive ingredient in the world of clay known as positive self-esteem, 3" x 21" x 25".

Using the Medium

Hand-built forms must be joined and constructed carefully if they are to survive the shock of a fast firing and the pressure of the tongs. The ten to fifteen percent shrinkage of clay as it dries must also be considered. When forms or supports are used, a newspaper or cloth separator should be placed between the support and the clay. This allows for easy removal and prevents the clay from sticking and eventually splitting as it dries. If a piece has not dried properly—that is evenly and slowly—it could crack or break. If the piece is too thick or if it is not thoroughly dry it might explode during the bisque firing. Special weight, size, and form limitations exist for raku ware because it must fit easily into the kiln and be easy to grasp and move with tongs; remember, it is to be removed from the kiln when still glowing hot.

I do not ask my students to create traditional Japanese tea bowls with the raku clay anymore than I could ask them to dress in a traditional Japanese kimono. What I do ask is that they work and create from their own instinctive feelings and innermost convictions. They need not turn to the standards of beauty or the values of another place and another time

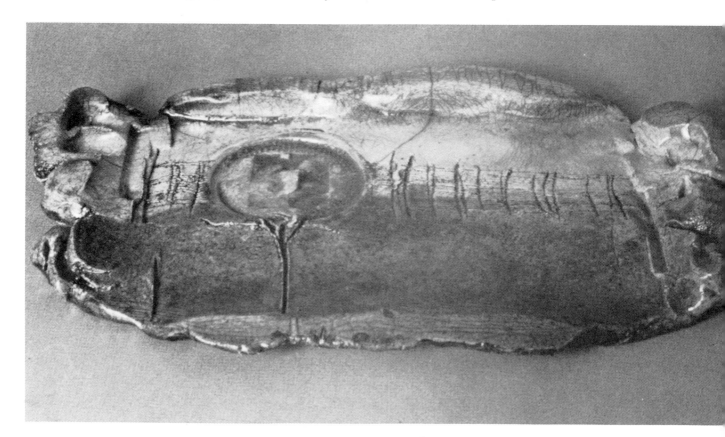

John Loree, hand built raku platter with incised design, 9" x 16".

Ed Risak continuously seeks to create a harmonious statement in form and glaze, 15'' tall.

to work in raku clay. However, I do encourage them to look at, admire, and study the pottery of other times, and the lives and philosophies of the creators of raku. It will not only serve as a source of stimulation, but it will make them more aware of the purpose of their own activities and their own lives.

An understanding and historical knowledge of the Japanese tea bowl can contribute immeasurably to the character of one's own work. To recognize the value placed on the subtle irregularity of form—the undulations

Steve Olszewski, thrown form with lid, 18" high.

of the rim; the texture of the glaze; the shape of the shallow depression on the inside of the bowl;* and the hand-formed contour of the foot rim— will give insights into personal expression. To be in sympathy with the values placed on the tea bowl, to be sensitive to the feelings of touch, both on the lips as the tea is sipped, and in the hands as the bowl is held, is to be in unity with your own senses and inner dialogue and capable of working from your own personality. The spirit of the raku bowl is part of its shape and substance.

The realization of physical forms created from clay requires a concentrated and coordinated effort by the potter. This is especially true of raku pottery, as you will learn by experiencing the entire raku process.

* This depression was used for holding the last droplets of tea, sometimes, for measuring to determine the amount of powdered tea needed to fill that bowl.

4

Glazes and Glazing

Raku glazes are like other ceramic glazes except they are designed to mature at temperatures between 1600°F. and 2000 F°., the temperature range of most present-day raku glaze bases. Raku glazes are usually classified by their fusion temperature, but may also be classified as raw or fritted, or as highly lead or highly alkaline in composition. Raku glazes may be opaque or transparent, depending on the presence and quantity of opacifiers or colored oxides. These glazes frequently have a glassy appearance and tend to craze or form crackly patterns upon cooling. If the crazing is undesirable, it may be remedied by the addition of flint (silica). Fluid melting and excessive running are characteristic of raku glazes, but this tendency can be overcome by adding a refractory such as kaolin.

The most pleasing characteristic of the low temperature raku glaze is the wide range of color, brilliance, and intensity possible from the various coloring oxides. Copper yields rich shades of green in oxidation (firing with an excess supply of oxygen) and many metallic lusters are possible in reduction (firing with a shortage of oxygen). Iron produces soft tones of tan and if a high percentage of the oxide is used, rich ambers and reddish browns will result. When small proportions of tin oxides are added as opacifiers the result is usually a warm creamy-looking glaze. Tin oxide imparts a pleasant softness to what might otherwise be harsh colors such as those that are made with the use of cobalt oxide.

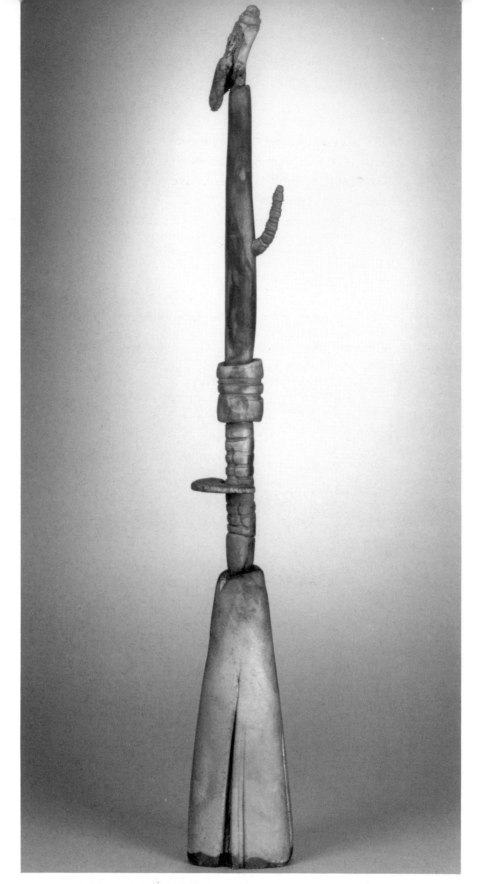

Robert Piepenburg, Twilight All Night, 31" high.

Lead Glazes

At one time, lead oxide was the most popular, if not useful, chemical in a raku glaze. As a flux it was the main ingredient. In fusions with the high-firing silicates (10% flint to 90% lead) it produced a glaze base capable of producing colors and effects unobtainable in any other glaze. The one big disadvantage to using a lead base glaze is that it is poisonous. It can be harmful to the potter

Douglas Wendyker obtains dramatic white crackle patterns by first applying several thin coats of white slip to the clay while it is still wet and on the wheel. After removing his pieces from the raku kiln he allows the "Mecham White" glaze to cool and craze one minute prior to placing it in the reduction container. After being in the container for one minute he "burps" the glaze (a process of temporally removing the lid and adding additional combustible). Pieces are burped 2 to 4 times, in one minute intervals, depending on the degree of definition and type of crackle pattern being sought.

who works with it and to those who eat or drink from ware glazed with it. Even if all of the safety precautions are taken when mixing and applying lead glazes, toxic vapors are still emitted at the kiln flu openings during firings.

Frit Glazes

Lead has been replaced by Gerstley borate (a natural colemanite) as the major flux in many raku glaze recipes. Commercial frits are currently running a close second. Frits are a combination of soluble compounds fired together with silica under strict regulations and dramatically shattered during a rapid cooling. The resulting small glass particles are ground to a fine powder to form a safe and reliable low temperature glaze flux.

Frits offer dependable uniformity and control in glaze making. As a result, the majority of commercially prepared glazes are formulated around them. Fritting also eliminates some of the hazards and problems of working with raw chemicals . . . especially if you make a health conscious effort to only work with lead-free frits.

David Powell, wheelthrown forms with sandblasted polychromatic glazes, tallest piece is 19½".

Opposite page, Larry Shew, variation of a tea pot theme, 4" × 10" × 16½".

After the wet clay has dried, pots should be bisque fired before they can be glazed and raku fired. This is sometimes referred to as the first firing and because the pots are unglazed they may, with care, be stacked together inside the kiln.

Bisque Firing

Most glazing is done on bisque ware—ware that has already been fired once at about 1915°F or to pyrometric cone 05. Bisquing removes moisture from the clay and changes it from a plastic substance that is soluble in water into a brittle substance porous enough to absorb glaze yet hard enough to be handled safely.

Many potters, respecting the traditional raku concept of softness as a quality of appearance and strength, bisque at a low temperature, such as 1640°F, or pyrometric cone 010. If the temperature is any lower than this, the ware may have to be dampened before glazing to prevent an excessive absorption of the glaze by the porous clay. Other raku potters prefer a dense clay body and have safely bisque fired at temperatures as high as 2125°F or cone 2.

Raku is usually bisque fired in the oxidizing atmosphere of electric kilns, and care must be taken to raise the temperature very slowly, until color is visible. After color can be seen, the temperature may be safely increased about 250°F. each hour, until the desired temperature is reached. If the ware is bisque fired in a top loading electric kiln the lid should be closed and the peep holes in the kiln should be plugged before the switches are turned on and the firing is started. The fire burns away most of the organic impurities in the clay, especially in fire clays with a low mineral content and a high organic content. Leave the holes in the kiln plugged throughout the firing to reduce odors. The fumes from firing this type of clay can become noxious if the kiln or kiln room is not properly ventilated. However, if there is adequate ventilation, the peep holes should be left open for the first few hours of firing to allow moisture and chemical fumes to escape. One can leave the hinged top of the kiln partially or entirely open for the first hour or two; this procedure also prevents rapid heating and lessens the chances of the ware exploding if you are firing thick or large, heavy pieces.

Should the bisque kiln overfire and the clay vitrify and become non-absorbent, it will make glazing difficult. Syrup or commercially powdered gums can be added to the glaze. These enable the glaze to adhere to the ware; they will evaporate and burn away during the glaze firing.

Gums are sometimes added to keep the glaze from chipping or flaking off the ware, but if a potter is reasonably careful when handling his glazed pieces, the use of gum can be avoided. Gum might also be added to a glaze that is going to be used over an already glazed and fired area. However, gum is usually unnecessary if the reglazing is done with a glaze containing a high percentage of clay, or if it is done right after the firing, when the pot is hot enough to hold the new glaze by causing the immediate evaporation of the water that is in the glazing solution. Raku pots can be reglazed and refired several times, but with each succeeding firing the chance for breakage multiplies. Reglazed pieces have a better chance for survival if they are refired immediately while still warm from the previous firing. If they have cooled, it then becomes safer to refire them at a later time when they can be included in the first firing of a cold kiln.

Some raku potters eliminate the separate bisque fire and fire glazed greenware to maturity in their electric or gas kilns. They slowly bring the temperature up to about 1700°F. over a five or six hour period. This one-fire method is the exception, however, and I only mention it because it calls for adjustments and adaptations in the glaze formulas. These adaptations are necessary because clay—especially greenware—and glaze expand and contract at different rates when heated. Most raku glaze formulas that are adapted for a single firing contain ten to twenty percent bentonite, or twenty-five to thirty-five percent ball clay.

Preparing the Glaze

Glazing raku is like glazing earthenware or stoneware pottery. Pieces can be glazed using the standard techniques—pouring, dipping, brushing, and spraying. Pouring, dipping, and brushing are the easiest methods to master, and require the least equipment. Spraying has many advantages but if the glaze contains lead, it has the disadvantage of creating a lead vapor or toxic atmosphere in a spray booth that is not adequately ventilated. A powerful exhaust fan must be used when spray glazing with a lead base glaze.

Raku glazes, like raku clay bodies, can be bought commercially prepared. However, if you want to save money and get closer to your craft, you might avoid them. There are times when exceptions might be .made: a few four-ounce jars of a brushing glaze that is applied in three coats, cone range 04 to 07, might be purchased to add a luscious tangerine, silver, or sanguine accent to a piece. It is often almost impossible to obtain such specific colors with your own glaze mixture, unless you resort to adding commercial glaze stains.

It is not particularly exciting nor fun to mix and make a batch of glazes, but it is easy and it involves the potter with ceramic chemicals and chemical formula calculations. The procedure simply requires the weighing out of each raw material—in grams, mixing the ingredients with water, and finally screening the entire solution through a 50 mesh sieve. Some of the coarser materials, such as granular borax or sodium uranate, may have to be added after sieving.

A quick and easy way to make up a batch of raku glaze is to recalculate the formulas so that the raw materials are added to the water by volume and not by weight—in a manner similar to using a cooking recipe.

The consistency of a glaze has a direct influence on color and surface texture. The glaze must be exactly right, resembling somewhat the pouring consistency of cream—thick enough to just reveal the outline of your fingernail when your finger is covered with glaze. Glazes should be stirred, mixed, or shaken before each use. The chemicals have a tendency to settle to the bottom in a matter of minutes leaving the water at the top of the container. Glazes that have not been used, but left sitting around the studio for a year or longer, should be tested by firing on small clay tiles and checked. The glaze materials may decompose and cause defects in the final glazed surface and color. I once reprocessed about 4,000 grams of a raku glaze that had stood unmixed for nine months. Additional water was

Marla Florio brushing commercial glazes on pendants that will be raku fired.

A previously raku fired pot being reglazed by the author after the original glaze was removed by sandblasting.

added, and then the glaze was stirred and resieved. The glaze was restored to the consistency of the original formula but the results were totally different from the glaze that was first used. Fortunately, it did work—in some ways it was more interesting than the original glaze—and did not have to be thrown out.

Applying the Glaze

The effects that can be obtained with glazes are limitless—each glaze can be changed with the use of slips, engobes, underglazes, stains, powdered oxide rubs, ochre washes, resists, and brush decorations.

The way the glaze is applied should be determined by the shape of the pot and the creative insights of the potter. The methods of glazing should not be thought of separately from the ceramic form to be glazed. Application and form should be indistinguishable. They work together as an entity—each holding fulfillment for the other. A form should not be dipped to cover it with a glaze, but should be dipped to compliment its contour and feeling. This may mean a quick splash into the glaze, or a gentle lowering at an angle. It may mean immersing the pot several times in the same glaze, or into glazes of different colors overlapping areas and exciting and subtle variations of color and shading.

The same is true in glazes that are applied by pouring—use a color and a technique that is compatible to the form being glazed. When pouring the glaze, it should be spontaneously cascaded on the clay form and allowed to freely follow and capitalize on its contour. If more than one coat of glaze is to be used, each coat should be applied when the preceding coat is still slightly damp. If the base coat of glaze is allowed to dry completely, parts of the glaze may crack and flake off, or still worse crawl in the firing.

Glazes that have been applied more thickly than one-sixteenth of an inch may run down the sides of the piece and form a pool inside. When this happens be sure that the piece is level while cooling. Thickly applied glaze may also drip down the outside of the piece to the foot and puddle on the kiln shelf. To keep the shelf and bottom of a pot free of runny glaze do not glaze three-quarters of an inch on the bottom of the pot. Wax or paraffin may be applied to the foot of a pot to prevent the foot from absorbing glaze. The wax will ignite and burn away as soon as the pot is placed into the hot kiln. Probably being very careful and neat when you apply the glaze and removing any excess with a clean, damp sponge is the best way to avoid glazed incrusted kiln shelves and pot bottoms.

Lusters

Some potters use metallic or lustery effects as part of their glazing. Lusters are light coatings of metal or metal oxides on the surface of the glaze. Iridescent sheens can be achieved in reduction immediately following the glaze firing, and come from metal oxides such as copper sulfate, copper carbonate, silver carbonate, bismuth sub-nitrate, and silver nitrate. Metal oxides may be applied to an already glazed but unfired surface by brushing

Dave Roberts, coil built bottle, 23″×22″ in diameter.

Richard Hirsch, Ceremonial Cup #29, 14½" high.

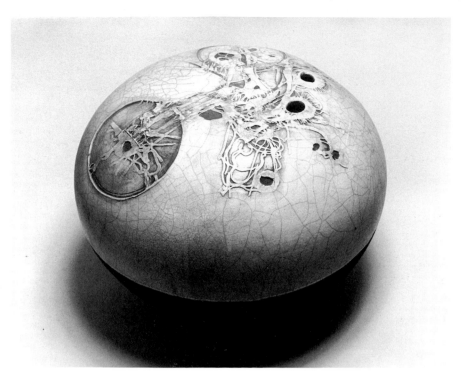

David Kuraoka, wheel thrown form with coil decoration, porcelain slip and a 50% colemanite - 50% nephaline syenite glaze.

or spraying before the glaze firing. Both lead and alkaline glazes can be used under lusters, although some darkening of color may occur if the glaze contains a great deal of lead or dark colorants. Metal oxides can also be added to the base glaze in small percentages. For example, two percent of silver nitrate can be added to a white glaze to obtain a gold luster. A different percentage of bismuth, sub-nitrate, or uranium oxide might also be added to the same glaze for a heightened reflective surface. For painted effects try a solution of 10 grams of silver nitrate to 50 cubic centimeters of water. However, this mixture must be used within a day or two after preparation—it weakens rather quickly. Many raku luster glazed surfaces have a tendency to fade if not vanish altogether months after the firing.

As you become more experienced and a more meaningful and intimate relationship with raku is established, you may well come to feel as I do that the black reduced clay body is beautiful in itself and in need of little or no glaze. However, raku is an individual matter. It has a strong tradition but holds no rigid rules or standard of values for individual self-expression, other than that feelings should be natural and honest. It would be very appropriate for the raku potter to develop a personal philosophy and approach toward glazing and not glazing.

Glaze Formulas

Several raku glaze formulas are given on the following pages. The base materials are listed first, and then the colorants are given. The glaze materials should be added to the water and then sieved. Glazes from these formulas have been used successfully as they are and in combination with other formulas. Each glaze matures at a slightly different temperature, and the results may not be exactly the same for every firing. This is due to human and mechanical variables, such as method of application, thickness of glaze, type of kiln, kiln temperature, reduction techniques used, and even weather. It is advisable to keep a glazing notebook and to include a quick but descriptive sketch of each piece with a list entry of the glze or glazes used and the way in which they were applied as well as the other variable factors.

RAKU SURFACE PATINAS: COR-TEN SERIES

(Note - These measurements are by volume and in the liquid state should resemble the consistency of very thin milk. The result, after post-firing reduction, should be a crusty metallic, semi-dry matt surface that is compatible with black body reduction and certain clay forms.)

Piepenburg Patina

4 parts Gerstley Borate
3 parts Bone Ash
2 parts Nepheline Syenite
1 part Copper Carbonate

Tin Can

4 parts Gerstley Borate
3 parts Nepheline Syenite
1 part Copper Carbonate
1/4 part Black Nickel Oxide

Michigan Patina

3 parts Gerstley Borate
1 part Cornwall Stone
1 part Nepheline Syenite
1/2 part Copper Carbonate
1/4 part Tin Oxide
1/8 part Black Nickel Oxide

Alligator

4 parts Gerstley Borate
2 parts Bone Ash
1 part Nepheline Syenite
1 part Copper Carbonate

Copper Sand

8 parts Gerstley Borate
2 parts Bone Ash
1/2 parts Copper Carbonate
1/4 parts Cobalt Oxide

Post-Pac-Man

5 parts Gerstley Borate
1 part Bone Ash
1 part Nepheline Syenite
1 part Copper Carbonate
1/8 part Red Iron Oxide

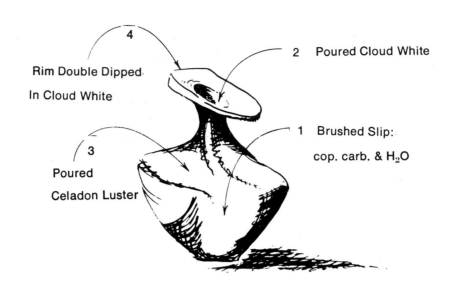

4 Rim Double Dipped In Cloud White

2 Poured Cloud White

3 Poured Celadon Luster

1 Brushed Slip: cop. carb. & H_2O

Sample sketch, as might be found in a glazing notebook, showing glazes used.

RAKU GLAZE FORMULAS

Cloud White

75% Gerstley Borate
25% Feldspar

Nantucket (Satin White)

45% Gerstley Borate
45% Nepheline Syenite
10% Flint

Smooth White Thunder

50% Nepheline Syenite
40% Gerstley Borate
10% Flint

Pearl White

56% Nepheline Syenite
44% Gerstley Borate

Hirsch White

40% Frit 3110 (Ferro)
40% Gerstley Borate
20% Nepheline Syenite
 8% Edgar Plastic Kaolin

Worthington

55% Gerstley Borate
30% Edgar Plastic Kaolin
15% Flint

Gibson

58% Gerstley Borate
26% Edgar Plastic Kaolin
16% Flint

White Rose

30% Gerstley Borate
30% Frit 3110 (Ferro)
18% Nepheline Syenite
10% Frit F142
10% Kaolin
 2% Tin Oxide

Piepenburg White

70% Gertsley Borate
15% Cornwall Stone
10% Tin Oxide
 5% Flint

Seattle White Slip

4 parts Ball Clay
2 parts Feldspar
2 parts Silica
1 part Kaolin
½ part Borax

Black Raku

44% Gerstley Borate
22% Soda Ash
19% Barnard Clay
11% Nepheline Syenite
 4% Cobalt Carbonate
 2% Copper Carbonate

Kuentzel Blue/Black/Purple

1 part Gerstley Borate
1 part Nepheline Syenite
1 part Copper Carbonate
1 part Rutile

Piepenburg Red Bronze

50% Gerstley Borate
45% Frit 3134 (Ferro)
 3% Tin Oxide
 2% Black Copper Oxide

OCC White

4 parts Gerstley Borate
1 part Cornwall Stone

OCC Luster

4 parts Gerstley Borate
1 part Cornwall Stone
⅛ part Copper Carbonate

Wood Ash Crackle

45% Gerstley Borate
35% Wood Ash
15% Flint
 5% Zinc Oxide

J.P. Metallic

65% Gerstley Borate
25% Anhydrous Borax
 5% Nepheline Syenite
 5% Kaolin
 5% Light Tone Rutile
 2% Black Copper Oxide

Lawton "G" Bisque Slip

25% Tennessee Ball Clay
20% Talc
15% Nepheline Syenite
15% Frit G-24
10% Soda Ash
 5% Flint

Douglas Dry

69% Red Copper Oxide
20% Bone Ash
10% Frit 3110 (Ferro)
 1% Cobalt Carbonate

Soldner Stain

50% Copper
50% Iron

Slip/Stain

1 part Ball Clay
1 part Frit 3124 (Ferro)
1 part Mason Stain

Joe's Stain

6 parts Gerstley Borate
2 parts Mason Stain
2 parts Nepheline Syenite
1 part Tin

Rosensus Slip/Glaze

33% Gerstley Borate
33% Nepheline Syenite
33% Copper Carbonate

Silver White Base

5 Parts Gerstley Borate

3 parts Nepheline Syenite

2 parts Lithium Carbonate

Donna's White

1 part Gerstley Borate

1 part Nepheline Syenite

1/2 part Superpax

Ivory White

1 part Gerstley Borate

1 part Cornwall Stone

1 part Nepheline Syenite

1 part Frit 3134 (Ferro)

1/4 part Superpax

White Mountain

60% Gerstley Borate

40% Potash Feldspar

  A-Payne's Gray

    1/4% Cobalt Carbonate

    3% Spanish Red Iron

Moon Base

75% Gerstley Borate

20% Flint

 5% Kaolin

  A-Winter Gray

    6% Umber

    8% Tin Oxide

Middlebrook's Crackle White

60% Gerstley Borate

50% Potash Feldspar

22% Barium Carbonate

16% Silica

Hank's Raconeat

55% Gerstley Borate

20% Nepheline Syenite

15% Lithium Carbonate

 5% Kaolin (E.P.K.)

 5% Tin Oxide

Smoky Metal

40% Gerstley Borate

30% Frit 3134 (Ferro)

20% Flint

 5% Ball Clay

 5% Whiting

Mecham White

80% Gerstley Borate

20% Cornwall Stone

  A-Deep Purple

    4% Manganese Dioxide

    1% Cobalt Oxide

  B-Carey's Copper Penny

    8% Ochre

    2% Black Copper Oxide

    1% Cobalt Oxide

  C-DelFavero Luster

    2% Copper Carbonate

  D-Gold Luster

    2% Silver Nitrate

    1% Tin Oxide

  E-Dragon Gray

    1% Red Iron Oxide

    1/4% Cobalt Carbonate

Hirsch Oribe Green

38% Frit 3134 (Ferro)

38% Gerstley Borate

19% Calcined E.P.K.

 3% Iron Oxide

 3% Iron Chromate

 2% Chrome

 2% Nickel Carbonate

 1% Potassium Bichromate

Hendry Base

50% Gerstley Borate

50% Borax

Soldner Base

80% Gerstley Borate

20% Nepheline Syenite

Conch White

4 parts Gerstley Borate
1 part Cornwall Stone
1 part Bone Ash

Hampton Satin

3 parts Gerstley Borate
1 part Cornwall Stone
1 part Custer Feldspar
1/2 part Bone Ash

Hines Patina

7 parts Gerstley Borate
3 parts Bone Ash
2 parts Nepheline Syenite
1 part Cornwall Stone
1 part Copper Carbonate

Yellow Iron

4 parts Gerstley Borate
2 parts Bone Ash
1 part Nepheline Syenite
1 part Cornwall Stone
1/2 part Copper Carbonate
1/2 part Black Nickel Oxide

Ghost White

1 part Gerstley Borate
1 part Talc

Crusty Gray

3 parts Gerstley Borate
1 part Tin Oxide

Clement Dolphin Blue

7 parts Gerstley Borate
3 parts Bone Ash
2 parts Nepheline Syenite
1 part Cornwall Stone
1 part Copper Carbonate
3/4 part Colbalt Oxide

Jernegan's Crusty Copper

34% Borax
33% Gerstley Borate
33% Kaolin (E.P.K.)
15% Copper Carbonate
15% Nickel Carbonate

Dry Washed White

1 part Gerstley Borate
1 part Cornwall Stone
1 part Nepheline Syenite
1 part Bone Ash
1/2 part Zircopax

Dry Patina

1 part Kaolin (E.P.K.)
1/2 part Gerstley Borate
1/4 part Copper Carbonate

Copper Brick

80% Copper Carbonate
20% Frit 3134 (Ferro)

Jernegan Lithium

70% Lithium Carbonate
15% Bentonite
10% Cornwall Stone
 5% Borax
 A—Red Copper
    10% Copper Oxide

One relatively simple way to begin your experiments with color in a base glaze is to use the 50–50 color blend method; this requires fifteen test tiles made from your raku clay body. To make these tiles, roll a slab of clay that is a quarter of an inch thick, cut fifteen strips, 1 1/2" × 4" each, from this slab. The strips should be bent in the form of an L so they can stand upright in the kiln and then left to dry. Freestanding pinch tiles or tiles that are cut from a wheel-thrown tile ring are other types of tiles that might be easier for you to fashion and use.

A good way to keep a set of glazed tiles together for future reference is to string them on a short length of cord. If you want to do this, a hole, one-quarter of an inch in diameter, should be made through the top of each tile while it is leather hard and before it is glazed and fired.

The following procedure is a systematic dry-blend method for testing the color possibilities of metallic oxides or carbonates, alone or in combination, in a single base glaze formula. It is a procedure for testing a set number of colorants (of certain percentages) along with all of the possible cross blends between any two of them. The row of circles running across the top of the stepped chart is the base line. It should show five different colorants of various percentages or the same colorant as five different percentages . . . either way the choice is yours to make. The remaining rows show all of the existing 50/50 blend combinations of the original five colorants chosen.

50/50 Dry Blend Glaze Color Test

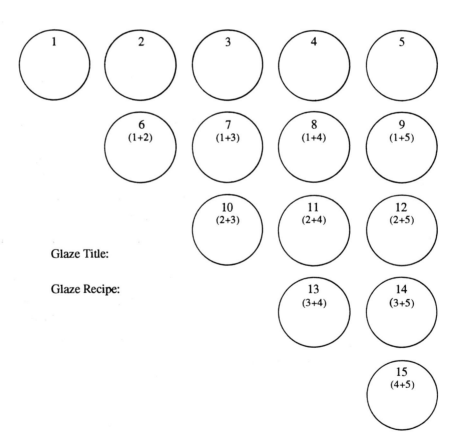

Procedure:

1. Choose the base glaze.

2. Choose the colorants and determine the percentages of each that you want to use.

3. Record this information on a chart similar to the one seen here.

4. Scratch this same information into the back of each test tile, when the clay is leather hard, along with the name of the glaze and the tile number.

5. Dry and bisque fire the tiles.

6. Number fifteen paper cups.

7. Make 500 grams of the base glaze; mix dry ingredients thoroughly.

8 Add 100 grams of the mixed glaze base to each of the first five cups.

9. Add the appropriate percentage of color to each of the first five cups and thoroughly mix the dry ingredients.

10. Add 20 grams of the mixture from cup 1 and 20 grams of the mixture from cup 2 to cup 6. Add glaze to the remaining cups in a similar fashion, taking care to assure that all combinations correspond with the information on the test chart.

11. Add water to the glaze in each cup. Adjust the consistency and screen.

12. Apply the glaze to the tile directly from the cup. Either pour or brush the glaze onto the top two-thirds of the front of each tile. Apply a second coating to the top one-third.

If tile #1 were to be glazed with a mixture containing 6 percent copper carbonate and tile #2 with a mixture containing 2 percent cobalt carbonate, tile #6 would be glazed with an equal mixture of 1 and 2; or a new glaze containing only 3 percent copper carbonate and 1 percent cobalt carbonate - because the amount of glaze base has been doubled the percentage of coloring carbonate is now reduced by one-half. So, if tile #6 is a success and if you want to mix a larger batch of this newly colored glaze, add only one-half of the tested colorant percentages (from the top row) to the base glaze.

The glazed tiles must be treated and fired in the same manner as other glazed ware. They should be completely dry prior to firing and only a few of them should be placed, along with a regular firing, in any one kiln load. If all fifteen of the tiles were fired at the same time, in the same kiln, the last few to be taken out might become too cool to respond to a post firing reduction.

5

Kilns

Raku kilns, like other kilns, are structures designed to accumulate heat. The heat may originate from a resistance and be radiated as it is in electric kilns, or it may come from the combustion of a fuel mixed with air or oxygen as in wood burning or gas kilns.

Kilns are usually constructed of materials that are resistant to heat and that will act as insulators, keeping the heat within the kiln.

Kiln Materials

The structures themselves can be built from any number of fire-resistant refractory materials, and can be constructed in a variety of shapes. Bricks are made from compounds of refractories, and are the most common structural material used, so most kilns are built in a variation of the box shape. Kilns are often designed to use standard-size bricks with a minimum of cutting. The standard brick shape is the nine inch straight which is a brick 2½" x 4½" x 9".

Most designers and builders of raku kilns choose either soft insulating

Steve Branfman, firing in a kiln built of hardware cloth and fiberfrax lo-con felt made from alumina silica fibers.

Wood fired kiln on the beach at Pescadero, California. The two-part removable top section is made from castable refractories. Castable materials often hold-up better than most bricks and can be cast into unusual shapes. Note how the opening of the fire box was positioned to take advantage of off shore winds.

Wood fired kiln with liftable top,
Wadell Creek, California.

Double chamber wood fired kiln.

*Fiberfrax kiln with expanded metal fram
The fiberfrax insulation material comes
rolls, is light in weight and is easily cv*

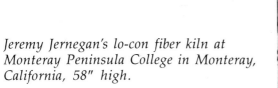

*Jeremy Jernegan's lo-con fiber kiln at
Monteray Peninsula College in Monteray,
California, 58" high.*

Rachel Porter's VW car kiln at a Pescadero Raku Festival. The gutted 1973 Volkswagen Beetle is fired by two venturi propane burners entering through the side panels. The front seat is the firing chamber, the back seat is a warming compartment and they are loaded through the windows. The front trunk is used as a reduction chamber while the engine compartment serves as a barbecue pit.

Hiroshi Kawashima's portable hinged fiberfrax kiln in San Francisco, California.

A four station natural gas hook-up with quick-release fittings. Each branch has its own shut-off valve, the main valve is located just under the regulator and is pictured in the on position (parallel to the gas line). The second stage regulator is set to reduce the inlet pressure of the gas service to an outlet pressure of 8" WCP (water column pressure) at the burner. The tongs with the shorter handles (center of photograph) are manufactured and sold by Hawaiian rakuist Ken Kang—four pointed prongs provide for an exceptionally secure grip on a variety of clay shapes.

Fiberfrax kiln with steel armature custom designed and built by John Murphy to raku fire large conical shapes. Note the use of a commercial weed burner.

Paul Soldner (the gentleman wearing the bowler) lowering his oil-fired fulcrumed kiln.

Members of the Fort Shafter Group rakuing on the beach at Kualoa Regional Park. Each year the Hawaii Craftsmen sponsor the RAKU HO'OLAULE'A: a three day, around the clock, raku firing event that goes a long way towards honoring the spirits of Earth, Fire and Water in a very charged way and in a very special place. Works fired at the Ho'olaule'a are juried on the afternoon of the final day for a major exhibition to be held later in Honolulu.

firebrick or ceramic fiber blanket. The fiber is available in 4, 6 and 8 pound densities (the 8 pound provides the greatest durability) and can be purchased in rolls that are 25 feet long and 2 feet wide (enough for two raku kilns). Fixed to an expanded metal (diamond shaped mesh) framework with clay buttons and short lengths of nichrome wire, fiber kilns are lightweight, portable and thermolly very, very efficient.

Soft or insulating firebricks are excellent materials for building raku kilns and are far more effective than other types of brick, due to a myriad of entrapped air bubbles. Raku kilns made of soft firebricks do not take nearly as long to bring up to firing temperature as do kilns made from hard bricks. This fact makes little difference in the quality of the glazes being fired, but it does affect fuel economics. It is difficult to say just how much heat loss is involved with hard brick vs. soft brick kilns. Temperatures as high as 600°F. can occur on the outside wall of hard brick raku kilns, whereas soft brick kilns with the same wall thickness will register temperatures only half as high. These soft firebricks are numerically rated according to temperature: a number 20 brick will function at 2000 degrees Fahrenheit. The number is a temperature service rating and not a service limit rating: a number 23 brick, for example, will not melt at cone 10 (2381°F).

Dave Deal removing large pot from kiln with special gloves and protective apparel.

Dave and Boni Deal, maple leaf imprint urn,
22″ × 32″.

Michael Hough, Industrial Innards with Figure, tile mural 19″ × 45″.

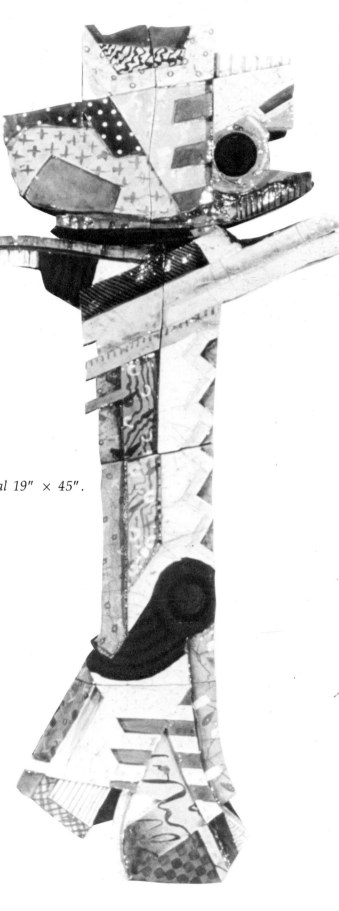

Some of the best, and I really mean best, gas fired raku kilns are made from old or used electric kilns. Switches and elements are removed, a 4 1/2 inch diameter flue hole is made in the lid and a burner port is cut through the side; level with the top of the floor. It's important that this opening be large enough to allow the burner to be positioned almost tangent to the inner curve of the wall. This way the flame is made to travel in a circular path around the wall, thereby eliminating the need for shelving. If you purchase a new electric kiln for bisque firings, make sure that it has at least one removable collar or ring—in time it may be reclaimed and be born again as a serious raku kiln.

The Fuel

More and more potters prefer to raku fire in electric kilns. It is hard on the elements but the distribution of heat is extremely uniform!

Wood burning kilns are appreciated and valued by many and have a Japanese heritage. Like charcoal burning kilns, they require a great deal of time and effort to fire, and produce a lot of smoke.

Fuel oil is relatively inexpensive, but dirty and smelly. It is a liquid which must be converted into a vapor before combustion can take place, which makes it difficult to start a fire and keep it burning until red heat is reached.

Natural gas works well as a fuel and should be used if the kiln is located near a gas meter. If you are not near a meter it can be expensive to have the utility company install a line and an additional meter. However, once the pipe and the meter are installed, it is much cheaper and safer to use natural gas than to use propane gas. If you fire with natural gas you never have to worry about losing pressure or running out of fuel during a firing. Natural gas kilns fire well when the gas is blended with forced air obtained from such sources as old or used vacuum cleaners or portable hair dryers. The air and gas lines can simply be laid adjacent to one another at the mouth of the burner port or, better yet, the gas line can be bent, positioned, and centered in the path of the air flow. Propane gas is a liquified petroleum gas that is delivered, stored in, and used from tanks that always seem to need refilling. Another problem during the operation of the tanks is that gas is continually being created by the vaporization of the liquid. If too much liquid evaporates into gas at one time, the remaining liquid in the tank freezes because of the temperature drop that accompanies evaporation; when this happens, pressure is lost.

To insure enough pressure, especially if you fire very often, 100-pound tanks should be used preferably in tandem. Each 100-pound tank should provide eight to ten hours of firing. If you have trouble during a firing, enough pressure to finish the firing can usually be obtained by turning a freezing tank on its side. This trick is very useful if there are no back-up or reserved tanks. Although there are many problems with vaporizing propane gas, I prefer it as a source of heat for firing my raku kilns.

Propane, unlike natural gas, is heavier than air. If a leak should occur around a hose fitting or at a tank valve, as has happened to me on two occasions with newly delivered tanks, the gas will collect and cling near the ground. Because of this, the tanks should not be located indoors or within twenty or thirty feet of basements or other sunken enclosures. If the tanks are to be stored in a specially designed outbuilding or shed, air vents should be installed at floor level. Local codes and safety regulations do exist, and your supplier should know what they are and be able to advise you on the building and ventilating of any enclosure you choose.

The Burner

You can buy burners, regulators, gauges, spark lighters, high pressure hoses, and fittings from most propane suppliers. The propane burners I designed for my own use were made from black iron pipe fittings that can be found in most hardware stores for one-fourth the cost of commercially made burners. The flange burner makes use of two one and one-half inch flanges, which are separated by flat washers, and provide the air needed for the proper combustion of the gas. The half-inch gas pipe enters the flange and is held in place by a reducing bushing with three equally spaced

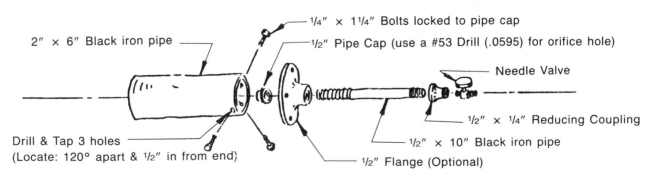

2" × 6" Black iron pipe

1/4" × 1 1/4" Bolts locked to pipe cap

1/2" Pipe Cap (use a #53 Drill (.0595) for orifice hole)

Needle Valve

1/2" × 1/4" Reducing Coupling

1/2" × 10" Black iron pipe

1/2" Flange (Optional)

Drill & Tap 3 holes
(Locate: 120° apart & 1/2" in from end)

Propane Burner

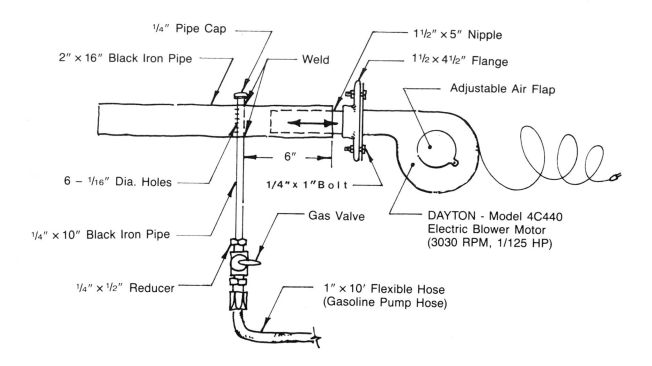

1/4" Pipe Cap

2" × 16" Black Iron Pipe — Weld

1 1/2" × 5" Nipple

1 1/2 × 4 1/2" Flange

Adjustable Air Flap

6 – 1/16" Dia. Holes

6"

1/4" × 1" Bolt

1/4" × 10" Black Iron Pipe

Gas Valve

DAYTON - Model 4C440
Electric Blower Motor
(3030 RPM, 1/125 HP)

1/4" × 1/2" Reducer

1" × 10' Flexible Hose
(Gasoline Pump Hose)

Natural Gas (forced air) Burner

A lid and two brick collars (recycled from old electric kilns) were simply placed upon a brick pad to make this exceptonally operative gas fired raku kiln. As with many things in life, the subtly simple things often miraculously become the best or most valued.

If attached to the propane tank, a high pressure regulator and 30-pound gauge will allow the potter more control in the firing of his kiln.

Natural gas forced air burner with electric blower. The Dayton electric blower motor slides out of the burner pipe so that it can be removed and brought indoors separately.

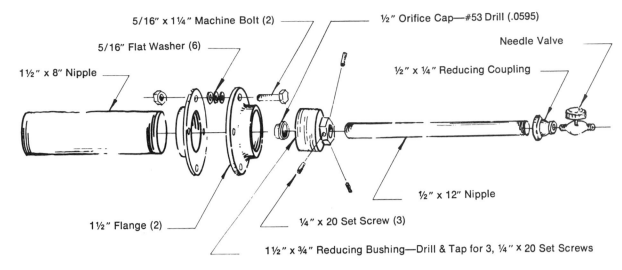

5/16" x 1¼" Machine Bolt (2)

5/16" Flat Washer (6)

1½" x 8" Nipple

½" Orifice Cap—#53 Drill (.0595)

Needle Valve

½" x ¼" Reducing Coupling

½" x 12" Nipple

¼" x 20 Set Screw (3)

1½" Flange (2)

1½" x ¾" Reducing Bushing—Drill & Tap for 3, ¼" x 20 Set Screws

Propane Flange Burner

Ben Pearlman, a prolific rakuist, never fails to savor the ecstasy of those moments when work is removed from the kiln and placed in reduction. As many of us know, anticipation and expectation warm the creative spirit and spontaneously revitalize the enjoyment of the raku drama . . . even on the snowiest of mornings.

set screws. The gas pipe is fitted—at the closed end—with an orifice made from a drilled pipe cap.

By varying the number of spacer-washers between the flanges, the air intake can be adjusted. If several washers are used a strong oxidizing atmosphere is created and the burner will draw in more than enough air, which means a hard and hot flame, and more heat. The same effect can be achieved by using an orifice made with a smaller drill. If a large orifice were used, a strong reduction atmosphere would exist because there would be a higher proportion of gas to air than needed for effective combustions. The flame would then be soft and cool. The position of the gas pipe is made adjustable by the use of thumb or set screws so that the orifice can always be set and secured just ahead of the air inlet should it be readjusted. This type of flexibility is helpful with homemade burners since some experimenting, adjusting, and even readjusting, usually has to be done. An additional advantage is that the orifice size can be quickly, easily, and inexpensively changed by simply replacing the drilled pipe cap. By increasing the diameter of the orifice hole in the pipe cap this burner can be efficiently used with natural gas.

To insure against gas leaks, all pipe joints, up to and including the orifice cap, must be coated with pipe dope or Teflon pipe tape and securely fastened. The brass needle valve connecting the burner to the hose is optional, but if it is used, the joint between the brass and iron fittings must be covered with dope. The brass to brass, or valve to hose-fitting joint, is of the same material and self-sealing and needs only tightening.

If you are nervous about lighting gas burners or in fear of flame failure you might want to consider adding a solenoid valve or a manual gas safety valve. Activated by a thermocouple, and used in conjunction with a pilot light for safer burner lighting, the supply of gas is automatically shut off should the pilot flame go out.

A Good Location

Before construction of a kiln can begin, a suitable location must be found. The kiln site is important in that it can, like weather, play a big role in setting the mood for the entire firing experience. It is, by far, a more rewarding and enriching experience to raku fire your ware in a kiln situated on a sandy plateau in the fields, in a wooded glen, or near a stream, than to fire in a garage or a cluttered alley. (Although I must admit that I have had some good pots and treasure some happy memories from firings done in, of all places, a Detroit junkyard.) The experience of firing frequently transcends the act of waiting for a kiln to reach maturing temperature for unloading. The firing often approaches an interrelatedness not only with one's pottery and every other part of the creative process, but with all things, from the murmur of the summer wind near the kiln, to the murmur of the sense of life within ourselves.

If the kiln is in a location where there are a minimum of unwanted and unnatural distractions to resist, the entire experience should be very pleasant. Attention can openly be given to the moment, whether it be one of silence, of conversation or a thought on life. Many memorable moments can be had with friends and refreshments during a firing session, whether it be early morning, late afternoon, or in the evening by gas lantern if the setting and atmosphere are right.

The inner experiences of raku are best enjoyed in the exterior settings of nature. The location of the raku kiln site should be more than just a practical matter.

The light-weight removable top of this raku kiln is made from ceramic fiber and metal mesh. The supporting walls are formed by two extension rings salvaged from discarded electric kilns. Two propane burners, fire in opposite directions to provide an even and efficient firing. Note the use of a pyrometer . . . a greater number of rakuists have come to depend upon them. While many experienced rakuists have developed an eye for judging the interior temperature of a kiln by the color of the pottery, others will lay a large ceramic firing cone (05) on top of a brick, leaving half of its length extended over the edge. The bending down of the cantilevered tip serves as a signal that the desired temperature has been reached.

Building the Kiln

The ground itself can serve as the foundation for a raku kiln. However, it may be wiser to support the kiln on a raised foundation made from hollow concrete blocks. If the kiln is built outdoors, a foundation will keep the mud and rain away from the lower part of the kiln. If the kiln is built indoors, on a concrete slab, hollow concrete blocks provide an air space that prevents the heat of the kiln fire from dehydrating, cracking, or, in extreme cases, causing the concrete slab to explode. If bare ground

Building the walls of a raku kiln with stringer courses of soft brick. Note the absence of mortar between the overlapping joints. Soft insulating bricks are accurately cut into a uniform size and can be used without mortar, whereas hard fire bricks are cast shapes and vary in the size and squareness. Frequently they require a water-fire-clay-sand mortar mixture to fill the joints and level the courses.

is used as a foundation for the kiln walls, it can also serve as the floor for the kiln, but if concrete blocks are used one or two layers of bricks are needed for the kiln floor. These flooring bricks prevent the concrete blocks from cracking and also act as insulators keeping the heat inside the kiln.

Soft bricks for the kiln wall are laid without mortar and are held in place by their own weight. An interlocking and stronger wall is obtained if the joints are alternated or staggered so that the bricks do not align. At times it may be necessary to use half bricks to achieve this overlapping at joints and corners.

Soft brick can be cut in half with a carpenter's ripsaw in a matter of seconds using another brick as a guide to get them cut in half evenly. Hard brick has to be scored, especially at the corners. Once it is scored it can be broken using a mason's chisel and a sharp hammer blow.

When it comes to determining the design for a kiln you should plan for quick and easy removal of the ware. If pieces are not removed immediately after the kiln is opened they will oxidize, and reduction in the post firing will not succeed. Car kilns and liftable drum-like kilns are good because the ware is accessible from all sides and from above the kiln. Small kilns with room for one or two small pieces work best, but if the kiln is large enough to fire several pieces at once, it should have the widest door or opening that is possible.

A used electric kiln converted into a gas-fired raku kiln. The small piece of kiln shelf is positioned to direct the flame away from the pottery and in a circular path along the interior wall. Shelving is unnecessary . . . pots are placed on the floor or a brick if desired.

Bob Smith, Colorado Pyramid, 9" x 9" x 29".

The round kiln under construction here is made from #1 and #2 insulating arch brick. Bands of metal strapping will be used to tightly hold each circular course of bricks together. The removable lid will be made from light-weight ceramic fiber blanket attached to a metal mesh backing.

If a standard size commercial kiln shelf is used, the design of the kiln should provide for one or two inch minimum clearance on all sides of the kiln between the shelf and the walls. Hard fire bricks work equally as well and have the added advantage of being economical to replace. Shelves are normally supported at a height of four and one-half inches above the floor of the kiln.

Burner ports are usually four and one-half or five inches square and are built to be level with the kiln floor. When possible they should be made to face into the prevailing wind, which will act as a blower and, on very windy days, help to save fuel. The burner itself does not actually go into the opening but remains just outside where it can be cooled by the incoming secondary air. If the burner was inserted into the kiln opening, the part that was inside the kiln would eventually burn and melt.

Care should be taken so that the flame does not come in direct contact with any of the ware; and the flame should be deflected by bricks, muffles, or clay saggers. If it is more convenient, the flame can be directed beneath a kiln shelf.

When designing or building a gas fired raku kiln, the size and location of the flue must be given careful consideration. Although this important aspect of the design is overlooked by many raku potters, it is a critical, if not the determining factor to successful glaze reduction. A flue opening is too large, for example, if the copper bearing glazes continually come out an oxidized green instead of a sumptuous copper looking metallic luster and remain so even after the post-firing reduction. On the other hand, a flue opening is too small if the kiln takes an unusually long time to fire to maturity and/or the pottery is covered with a dark carbon soot which can, incidentally, be burned off in three or four minutes by simply moving the kiln door or lid slightly to create a secondary flue opening. If a fixed flue size is too large and does not give good results with a particular kiln design some creative activity and experimentation may have to be done with a damper. The damper need not be anything more than a hard brick or a piece of broken kiln shelf used to cover or restrict the flue opening as needed. The damper might be used much in the same way it is used with gas fired stoneware kilns: the flue may be left uncovered during the early stages of the firing cycle to maintain an oxidizing atmosphere and rapid rise in temperature and partially or entirely covered during the final stages of the firing to obtain a reducing atmosphere within the kiln. A reducing atmosphere exists within the kiln when the flue opening is covered enough to restrict the draft or draw off oxygen at the burner port. Proper flue restriction during reduction should force a small but visible flame to

Ken Kang's oil drum kiln with a homemade, swing-away, forced air burner. The drum is cut into three sections to provide for an extension collar and removable lid. The ceramic fiber is attached with sodium silicate and stainless steel bolts and large fender washers.

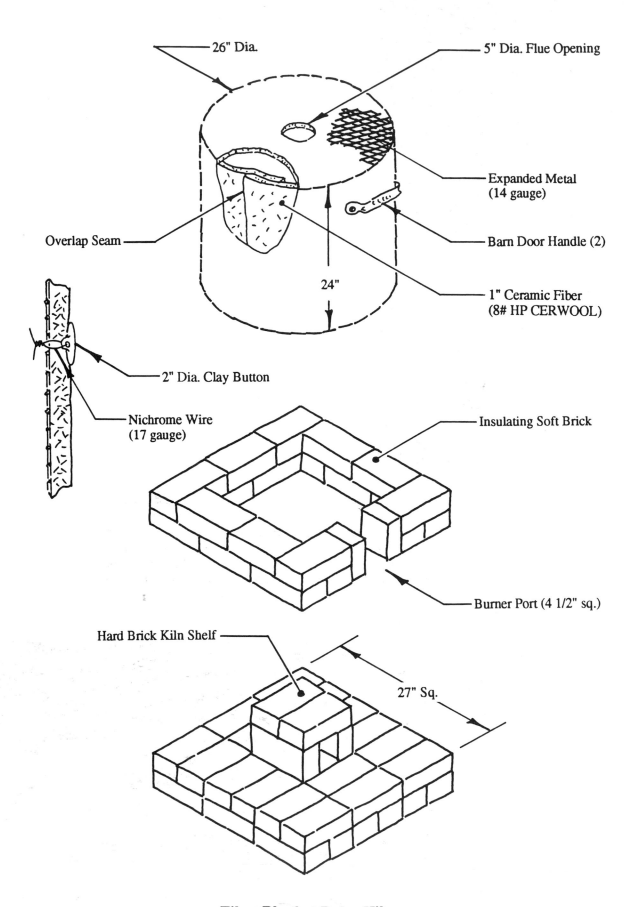

26" Dia.

5" Dia. Flue Opening

Expanded Metal
(14 gauge)

Overlap Seam

Barn Door Handle (2)

24"

1" Ceramic Fiber
(8# HP CERWOOL)

2" Dia. Clay Button

Nichrome Wire
(17 gauge)

Insulating Soft Brick

Burner Port (4 1/2" sq.)

Hard Brick Kiln Shelf

27" Sq.

Fiber Blanket Raku Kiln

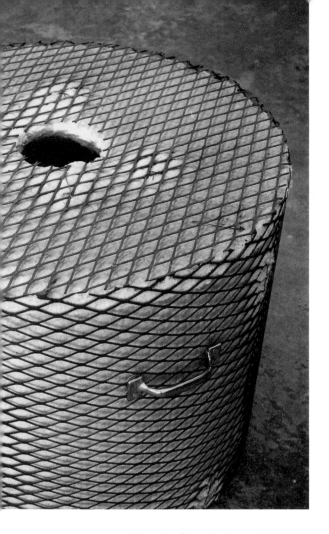

The 1" thick knitted CERWOOL fiber blanket is attached to the welded metal frame by 30 handmade buttons. Two holes could have been bored through the buttons to accommodate the high-temperature wire but only a single hole is needed if the finger-end of a wood modeling tool is pressed into the soft clay to form a raised wall on the back of the buttons. Buttons may also be extruded in the shape of a modified "T" and cut into 1 1/2 inch lengths. A single hole made in the leg of the "T" prevents the wire from being directly exposed to the interior heat of the kiln.

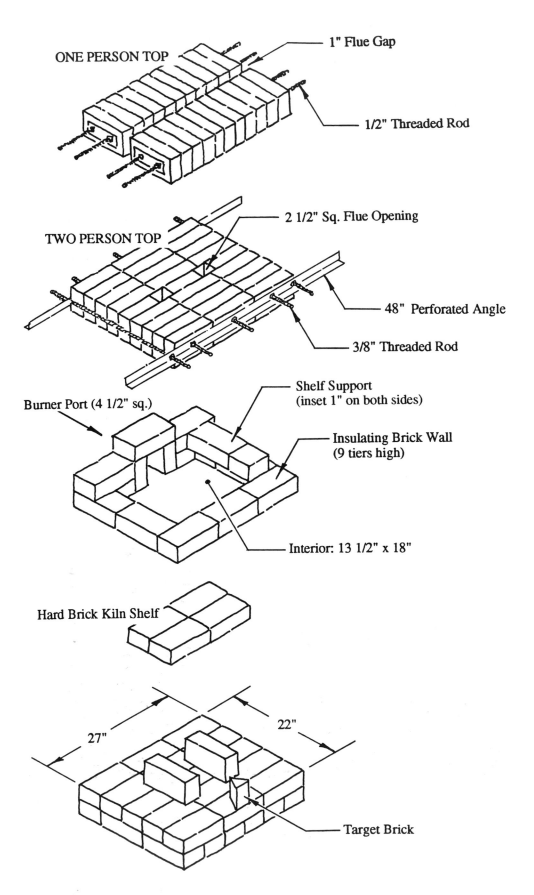

ONE PERSON TOP

1" Flue Gap

1/2" Threaded Rod

TWO PERSON TOP

2 1/2" Sq. Flue Opening

48" Perforated Angle

3/8" Threaded Rod

Burner Port (4 1/2" sq.)

Shelf Support
(inset 1" on both sides)

Insulating Brick Wall
(9 tiers high)

Interior: 13 1/2" x 18"

Hard Brick Kiln Shelf

27"

22"

Target Brick

Top Loading Raku Kiln

shoot out any remaining flue opening and the burner port. Often, all that is needed for a reduction firing in a raku kiln is thirty to sixty seconds of reduction (brick over the flue) followed by thirty to sixty seconds of oxidation (flue uncovered) at the end of the firing just before the kiln is opening and the ware removed.

Reduction is not difficult to achieve in a well made fuel buring kiln. It is simply a matter of starving the kiln of oxygen. Raku kilns that are poorly made, with large openings at the joints, cannot be sufficiently reduced in that they are literally one big flue. There can be no substitute for the beautiful reduction effects that can be had in a tightly made kiln. The erratic richness and unique brilliance of the reduced glaze produces much of the most satisfying and valued raku pottery. The reduction results can never be completely controlled, that is how it is and that in part gives each piece we make its unique presence and incarnation.

Removing a two person compression lid from a top loading kiln. Notice how the tongs for removing the ware are temporarily placed, for ready access, upon that part of the metal frame extended to serve as handles.

6

Firing: Metamorphosis

The glaze firing is the most exciting and dramatic phase of the whole raku experience. An understanding of the fire's powers of transformation coupled with a feeling for it and its capacities is needed if one is going to realize the full potentialities of raku pottery. The raku glaze firing holds a special place of honor in the potter's craft in that it allows potters to live with and experience every transforming phase. Potters can peer into the kiln's interior and in less than an hour observe the formation of the glaze; first as it begins to sinter in the early stages of melting, then as it goes through the bubbling stage, and finally when it reaches the molten liquid state, i.e. when bubbles disappear and fusion is complete. As knowledge is gained through experience, the kiln watcher is able to make small adjustments on the ware during the firing. They might observe an unexpected bare spot on the rim and by opening the door or lid be able to drop some powdered Gerstley borate on it with a long handled metal dipper, or they might suddenly decide to add a powdered metallic oxide to one area for additional color. Such judgments

Penelope Fleming, Sequent Flight, hollow walled forms glued onto an armature, 28" × 114" × 18".

Georgia Pozycinski, Fish Vessel,
wheel thrown with sculptured
addition, 16" tall.

Melissa Emery, with the aid of a pyrometer, fires her 90% copper / 10% frit glaze to 1860°F and then turns off the supply of gas to allow the kiln's temperature to drop to 1100 degrees before relighting the burner. When the temperature inside the kiln climbs to 1200°F the gas is again turned off and the pot promptly removed and placed, along with a handful of dried oak leaves, inside a garbage can for reduction. The reduction can is just slightly larger than the pot and, when the leaves begin to burn, is immediately covered with a lid lined with 4-8 full sheets of wet newspaper, double folded at the rim, to form a smokeless seal. Bowl, 5 3/4" x 14 3/4".

result from insights into the actions of fire and can have a direct influence on the success of a piece. Once again the opportunity of expressing ourselves creatively, even as we work with the firing, speaks of the potency of raku and its ability to reflect the wholeness of a person as one is able to express one self in all the phases of the creation of raku.

Everything—the digging of the clay; the preparation of the clay; the forming of the piece; the building of the kiln; and the firing of the bisque, is a prelude to the drama of the glaze firing. The anticipation is present in every phase of raku pottery making. When the clay body is composed, the fact that the ware will have to undergo drastic changes—going from a cold environment into a hot one, and then immediately back to a cold one—without breaking, is a consideration in the mixture of the clay body itself.

The clay body and the bisquing temperature of raku ware is determined by the final firing; if the bisque temperature is too high, the ware will lose its porosity and may break in the glaze kiln.

The shapes of the pots are created and designed for the firing. The pots must be made in shapes and sizes that will allow them to be easily placed in the kiln and removed from the kiln with tongs.

Reduction after the glaze firing is a recent American contribution to the raku process. Traditionally, the Japanese raku ware was either air-cooled or water-cooled after it was taken from the glaze kiln. This cooling process did little to alter the color of the bisque clay, and contributed little to the richness of the glaze. Most contemporary American potters either partially or fully reduce their pieces when they are removed from

J. T. Abernathy's large tumescent form was fired to 2000°F and while still in the hot kiln the gas was turned back to let the temperature drop to around 1400 degrees. The gas was then turned up and the temperature increased 150 degrees, while maintaining a heavy reduction atmosphere, before it was transferred to an external reduction container.

the kiln by placing them in an oxygen-free atmosphere while they are kiln-hot. The resulting reduction effects are magnificent—the clay body may turn to a smoky gray or jet black and the glazes might turn to metallic or iridescent lusters, depending on the metallic oxides or chemicals that are used.

In theory, reduction after firing is not very different from reduction during firing, as is often done with high fire fuel—burning stoneware kilns. When oxygen is in short supply, carbon and carbon monoxide are liberated during combustion and they chemically take oxygen from any other available source—such as the clay and the glaze materials. These materials are "reduced" when they are deprived of oxygen and the reduction affects their color. Reduction as associated with raku is usually a post firing treatment and is done at low temperatures allowing for a wide range of glaze colors that are not possible at high firing stoneware temperatures. The time involved is also very short so that the results are only on the surface in contrast to the penetrating effects in the reduction of stoneware.

As with high-fire stoneware kilns, a partial reduction atmosphere can be maintained inside of the raku kiln during the entire length of the firing or it can be initiated during the final few minutes by restricting the amount of "secondary air" entering the burner. A reudction atmosphere can also be initiated by simply limiting the size of the flue opening at the top of the kiln during the firing. If, however, the pottery is severely over reduced during the raku firing it will be covered with a dark black soot when the kiln is opened and, without being removed, should be immediately refired for several minutes within a neutral, non reducing, atmosphere to burn off the carbon smudge. I seldom reduce in the kiln anymore: it can make the white crackle glazes appear dingy and faded. I much prefer to obtain my surface finishes in a post firing reduction container that is tightly sealed by a soaking-wet piece of carpeting, heavy cloth or newspaper placed between the lid and the container or by inverting the container, placing it over the pot, and forcing its rim down on and into loose earth or sand. If the post firing reduction is done properly there should not be much smoke.

A well known Ann Arbor rakuist, J.T. Abernathy, generates so little smoke when he works that he is able to both fire his kiln and reduce his pots inside of his downtown studio. He also approaches his high copper-bearing glazes metallurgically, knowing that if they are going to have any permanence or lasting quality, they will have to be fired to at least 2000°F to become archivally set. This is especially important with recipes containing high percentages of copper.

Loading a cold kiln.

Loading the Kiln

The glaze firing can be a success only if the glaze melts and covers properly. The way the glaze is applied is determined by the firing. If a large section of the body is left unglazed, the reduced clay should turn black complimenting the surrounding glazed areas.

Glaze dampness causes more breakage during the firing than does any other single factor. Air bubbles in the clay and excessive thickness of the clay walls are often cited as factors in breakage, but to my knowledge they seldom, if ever, cause pieces to explode in the raku kiln. Poor construction and an overfired bisque also account for some breakage. The best way to keep pots from blowing up during the glaze firing is to make sure that they are absolutely dry before they are placed in the glaze kiln. The vehicle for glaze is water, and it must evaporate completely before the firing. Usually, the glaze must be applied at least a day before the firing of the kiln. If a piece were glazed just before it was placed in the

The author using tongs designed for removing tumescent ware from a top loading kiln.

kiln, it would almost certainly be damp, and would probably explode during the firing.

Some potters put their newly glazed ware into an electric bisque kiln leaving the lid open and the electric switches turned to low for about an hour before placing them into a hot raku kiln. Other potters pre-heat their glazed pots for several hours by placing them on top of a kiln that is being fired. Other potters include them in the first firing of a cold kiln, bringing the temperature up slowly. These methods are not completely satisfactory and I suggest you simply allow the glaze to dry overnight, or even longer if the weather is rainy or humid. After the glaze is dry, it certainly won't hurt to place the ware on the top of the hot or firing kiln for pre-heating as the pieces await firing. Pre-heating is not really necessary, but if no ware-board, or shelf for glaze ware storage, is available it is safer to store the ware on the top of a kiln than leave the glazed ware on the ground where it might pick up moisture, or be stepped on.

If by chance, a piece should explode and you hear it, open the kiln immediately and remove all the fragments. If other pots are being fired, the debris might fall and fuse to them, ruining everything in the kiln.

Pieces that are large, awkward to handle, fragile, or made from a stoneware body should be included in a first firing of a cold kiln. With bare hands, the pieces can be easily placed in the best position, thereby decreasing the chances for breakage by the tongs. Careful positioning of a piece also decreases the chances for breakage when the piece is removed with the tongs. A slow, gradual rise in temperature is also easier on most ware, particularly large pieces that have been constructed of many slabs that have been joined into one large piece.

Lighting a vapor propane torch from burning newspaper.

Jeff Hale preparing a hay reduction nest.

In loading the kiln you may find some pieces that have to be propped up with a brick, or leaned against the kiln wall. If a piece touches another pot, no great harm will result because the glaze will be fluid when the pots are taken from the kiln and the pieces will separate easily.

Platters, tiles, and flat pieces are best fired standing on edge and leaning against the inside wall of the kiln. They take up less room and are easily removed from this position. However, unusual glaze patterns might result from a running glaze, and you should be prepared for them. It is also much safer to fire large flat forms on end or propped up against a wall rather than resting flat on a shelf—particularly in a hot kiln. Kilns that have been firing for several hours, or whose lower shelves are near a combustion chamber become very hot and can cause cracking in and near the bottoms of the ware. Placing glazed pieces on a glowing hot shelf is too much of a heat shock for the new, cold ware. A solution for this problem is to pre-heat the ware or change the shelves, replace the glowing hot ones with preheated shelves that are slightly cooler. You couldn't use cold shelves because they would crack or blow up since they, too, would suffer from the thermal shock. The best solution is to shut the kiln down and allow it to cool for a half hour OR place a piece of broken soft brick between the cold clay piece and the hot shelf.

Different glazes will melt at different temperatures and you must make sure that all of the bubbles have disappeared before it is removed from the kiln. Or, in most cases, the bubbles will remain when the piece is cooled. At times it is wise to let a piece at the fluid-glaze stage remain in the kiln an extra minute or two at a constant temperature before removing it; this will assure uniform maturity. Depending upon the circumstances, glaze will usually melt on the inside bottom of the piece first and on the upper rim last. If the glaze is applied too thickly to a bowl form, it will puddle inside on the bottom; when that happens place the hot bowl on a level surface so that the glaze puddle will not cool and harden at an angle.

In firing a number of pieces, the kiln should be unloaded and reloaded again as quickly as possible. Working quickly saves fuel and time, and keeps the kiln at an even heat. Each succeeding load will require less time and less fuel. When the kiln is very hot a firing cycle may take as little as fifteen minutes. If you are doing a successive number of fast firings, be sure to place cool soft brick spacers between the hot shelf and each new clay form.

Removing the lid.

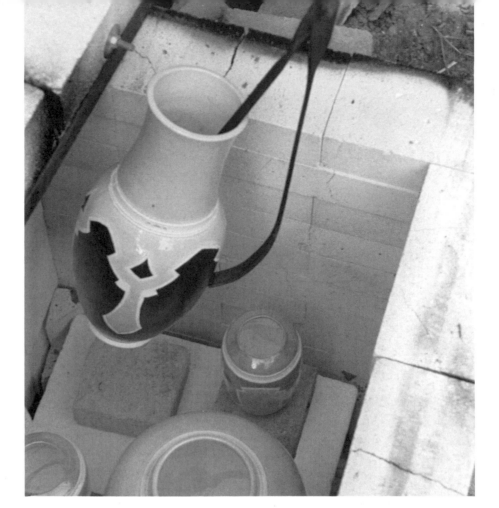

Removing the pot from a hot kiln.

Reducing in hay.

The Firing Cycle

The time required for the initial firing of a cold kiln depends on the size or type of kiln to be used. In most cases it should take less than an hour. If a piece is unusually large or complicated it might be placed in a cold kiln and fired slowly up to temperature over a period of two or three hours before being removed or reduced in place. Porcelain can even be fired successfully in this manner. The real thermo-shock to raku ware comes when a relatively cold piece is loaded into a hot kiln and not, as many believe, when the piece is brought from the kiln into a cold atmosphere.

In using vaporized propane for fuel I start firing with a pressure of ten pounds and after several firings, when the bricks have heated, I usually lower the pressure to anywhere from four to six pounds. When loading or unloading, the pressure is turned down even further, either at the regulator on the tank, or better still, at the needle valve on the burner, allowing just enough pressure to keep the flame from going out. More often than not, however, I turn the gas off completely, just prior to unloading the kiln. This not only saves fuel that might otherwise be wasted in an open kiln, but it is safer, and much more pleasant than working near a continuous wave of invisible heat.

Kiln shelves need to be removed and cleaned frequently, especially if you want a clean, well-reduced foot area on your pots instead of a foot that is caked with several different glazes and in need of grinding. If glaze does puddle on the kiln shelf, sand or grog can be sprinkled over the patch of glaze before the kiln is loaded. If hard bricks are used for a shelf, and become covered with glaze, they may be easily discarded and inexpensively replaced with clean new ones.

Using Tongs

Long handled tongs are generally used for removing the red hot glazed ware and for the placement of unfired glaze ware into the hot kiln. The tongs can be made from metal tubing, flat iron, iron rod, pipe, or any material that is handy or usable. The tongs that I use are fabri-

Elbow length leather welding gloves and home-made raku tongs. Easily shaped with a large pipe wrench and table vise, the tongs are formed from two lengths of flat iron ¹/₄" × ³/₄" × 48".

cated from hand-forged iron rod, three-eighths of an inch thick. They have round jaws that are three inches in diameter and handles that are three feet long. If you're lucky, you might be able to locate a blacksmith to fabricate a pair to your own specifications.

Tongs are simple to fashion and you can probably make your own for under ten American dollars. The third tape of my three tape video series on Raku documents this process in detail. Two four-foot lengths of one quarter by three quarter inch flat iron are bent and shaped with the aid of a large pipe wrench and a machinist's vise. The vise is used to form the desired curvature of the jaws.

Welding gloves can be used to hold the tongs, especially if you use a top loading kiln. Heat rises; when a top loading kiln is opened, you can easily burn your hands even when the very long-handled tongs are used. Welding gloves are also useful for picking up and moving still warm ware at the kiln's site, for lifting hot bucket lids, for adding a tier of bricks to raise the wall of a hot kiln, or to simply prevent burnt fingers.

The Reduction

The special aura that permeates the raku experience centers about the firing and yields itself to us at that moment when we reach into the open kiln with our tongs. That moment, more than any of the other growth stages of the raku pot, has the potential of revealing and truthfully illuminating our inner selves. In the few seconds that it takes to pick up the pot with tongs and remove the pot from the kiln, all the potter's experiences are directed at the ware and all are summoned into consciousness. All the preparation and previous activity are evaluated in terms of what is done in the next few moments. The personal commitment of the potter to his work and to himself is reflected in the way the potter handles each piece of raku while it is glowing in the jaws of the tongs.

Pieces that are going to be heavily reduced must be immediately taken from the hot kiln and quickly placed into an air-tight enclosure containing some dry combustibles. Sawdust, excelsior, shredded paper, leaves, and straw might be used as combustibles, and only a few handfuls of one of these materials is needed. The most effective air-tight enclosure is a hole dug in the ground and covered with an inverted metal trash can, or just the lid of the trash can, depending on the size of the piece to be reduced.

If a reduction container is not completely air tight or a great deal larger than the war, a large quantity of one of the dry combustibles is needed. The combustible material is placed at the bottom of the hole and the just-from-the-kiln piece is put in the hole on top of the sawdust, leaves, etc. The cover of the can is quickly placed over the top of the can or hole, making an air-tight enclosure and sealing the piece within. Additional combustibles such as straw or hay may be thrown on top of the ware, especially if there are large unglazed areas, and allowed to ignite before the cover is added. The results of the reduction depend greatly on the condition of the combustible material that is used; if the material is damp, coarse, or used, it will not burn well, nor provide much free carbon. However, the results of reduction done in a covered pit are usually strong and excellent because an almost completely air-tight seal is formed by the cover of the can and the ground, any oxygen is prevented from entering the hole and weakening the reduction.

Clay bodies turn a rich black and glazes with colorants turn to dark lusters in the smoky atmosphere. Some glazes become too dark and lustery in the pit and are better looking if they are held in the air for a few moments and allowed to oxidize and cool slightly before being reduced. Other glazes look best when not reduced at all and are left to oxidize on an open pile of sawdust so that just the exposed clay at the bottom of the piece gets a partial reduction.

It is sometimes wise to leave ware enclosed in the reducing atmosphere for about five to ten minutes while the ware cools. The glaze and clay body reduction will take place immediately, but the piece might re-oxidize and the reduction effects partially lost if the piece were allowed to cool in the open air after being reduced for only a short period of time. To avoid re-oxidation many potters quench their ware with water immediately after removing it from the reducing atmosphere. Instead of immersion into a container of water, I prefer to use a garden hose with an on-off nozzle handle. For good and lasting glaze reductions, raku pottery must be allowed to either cool in the reduction atmosphere or be cooled down with water immediately upon being exposed to the open air.

Interesting reduction effects can be achieved by burying a piece of ware either partially or entirely under a combustible fuel such as sawdust. If you use this technique it is usually a good idea to have the reduction fuel, especially sawdust, slightly damp, or combine with sawdust that has been reclaimed from another glaze firing session. This will not only prevent the entire pile of sawdust from flaming up, but it will also provide a tighter reduction seal around the form. A note of caution: liquid molten glaze that is buried with or comes into contact with the reducing material too soon will develop charred textures that can be rough and unattractive.

If you have fired a piece containing a white crackle glaze, and no copper carbonate, there is not a great urgency to pull it out immediately upon the opening of the kiln. By waiting a minute or so, the glaze will cool and harden a little, rendering it less responsive to the texture imprinting of the combustible material. To enhance the visual qualities of the surface fissure patterns, place the piece into a small metal container of sawdust, allow a healthy flame to develop, and quickly cover it with a metal lid. After a half of a minute, remove the lid, sprinkle a handful of dry sawdust on the piece, allow the sawdust to ignite and replace the lid.

Repeat this process one or two times more. The end result, depending upon the form, should be a great deal of smoked definition within the crackle crevasses themselves.

Another reduction scenario involving white crackle glaze might involve a newspaper fuming technique such as Jeff Hale is successfully using on page 146.

Copper Matt Glazes

Little by little, that captivating raku surface, the dry copper matt, is arousing, if not seducing, many raku potters. To be sure, they are alluring but they are also beguiling and difficult to obtain and to manage. Consider that these popular glaze surfaces are generally 70 to 90 percent copper with a little frit mixed in for control. Also consider that they have to be fired, at the very least, to cone 05 to become fortified. Otherwise they remain waywardly vulnerable to oxidation over a short passage of time and to human handling.

Temperamental as these glazes are, many rakuists have their own individual, if not reliable, methodology for working with them. Some spray the glaze on the pot before it is bisque fired; spray on an additional application after it is bisque fired then raku fire it to temperatures well below cone 05 prior to removing it from the kiln for a post-firing reduction in an air-tight container. Some rakuists are highly scientific in how they manipulate the post-firing reduction. They take great pains to open the container after an exact interval of time, say two minutes, add a little more combustible and continue the reduction for an additional amount of time, say precisely seven, nine or ten minutes (depending on the size or wall thickness of the pot) before cooling it down with a quick application of water. Still, others obtain dry matt surfaces through the use of underglazes and/or commercial stains mixed into clay slip and applied to the pot while it is still wet or leather-hard. Such finishes cannot be over-reduced or reduced for too long a time after firing, otherwise they become dark, if not black. In some cases rakuists completely remove the black carbon and restore the richness of the matt color by briefly torching the pot, while it is still warm, with the same gas burner they used to fire the kiln.

When glaze has matured and the ware is ready to be taken from the kiln you must make the decisions that will ultimately affect the final appearance of the form. Needless to say, no one else should ever fire your work. Not only would it oppose the spirit of raku, but it would deny the final moments of intimacy between the pot and the potter that culminate the creative experience.

Flames are allowed to peak before the pot is covered.

After one or two minutes of reduction the can is removed and the pot quickly covered with a loose dirt/sawdust mixture.

After several minutes sawdust is carefully removed with a stick and the exposed copper glaze surface is immediately squirted with water to arrest the color and prevent it from reoxidizing.

Cleaning off carbon build-up with a scrub pad.

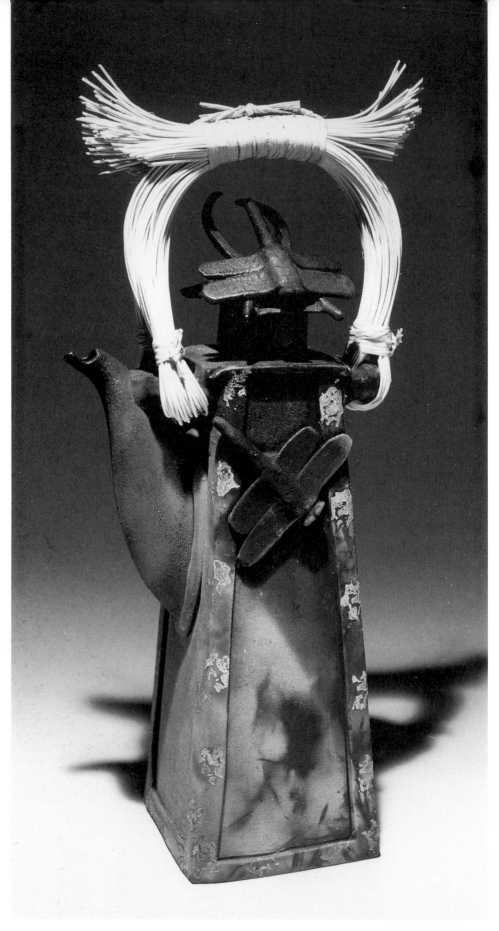

Gail Bakutis, Dragonfly Tea, assembled with leather-hard clay, 6" x 10" x 28".

Robert Reedy, Teapot and Table, decorated with slip and stain, reduced in sawdust, 18" high.

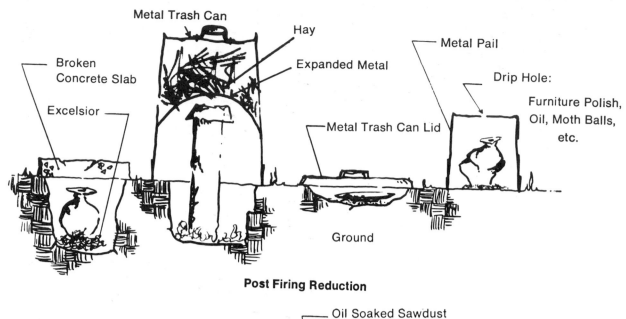

Broken Concrete Slab

Excelsior

Metal Trash Can

Hay

Expanded Metal

Metal Pail

Drip Hole:
Furniture Polish,
Oil, Moth Balls,
etc.

Metal Trash Can Lid

Ground

Post Firing Reduction

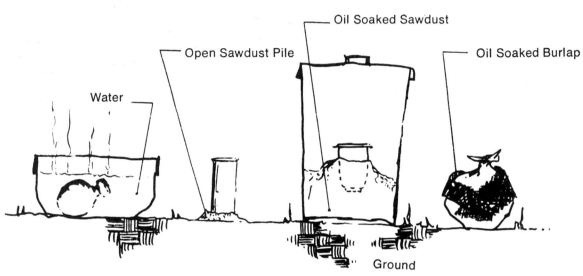

Water

Open Sawdust Pile

Oil Soaked Sawdust

Oil Soaked Burlap

Ground

Reduction container with intersecting steel rods that form a grid to hold these linear sculptures upright during reduction fuming.

Oil drums cut to various heights for placement over pottery during post-firing reduction.

Charlie Blossor's sand pit for post-firing reduction. Hot pots are placed on the ground inside a small nest of a combustible (such as straw or excelsior) and covered with an inverted container as soon as the flames peak. The rim of the container is pushed down into the sand to form an air tight seal (a "sand seal") that smothers the flame and eliminates smoke. The containers are not removed until the pots have cooled to a temperature below 100°F.

White crackel glaze placed in a reduction can. (Wait thirty seconds after removal from the kiln before reducing).

Adding more paper to create additional flames. (At one minute intervals further paper may be added . . . cautiously).

Adding lid with a newspaper gasket. (Gloves should be worn).

Securing an air tight seal for a heavy reduction.

The possibilities for raku pottery effects are many and new approaches will always develop as pot and potter grow and change through the experience of the fire. The uncertainties are many and fire can symbolize the warmth of love, or the wrath of an inferno. We, as potters, often stand humble before the power of the fire with our hopes both melting away and burning with anticipation, as they lie flickering in the flames of suspense. And, best of all, if the results are disappointing or unsatisfactory, the piece may be reglazed, while it is still hot, and, with high hopes, we can surrender it once again to the flames.

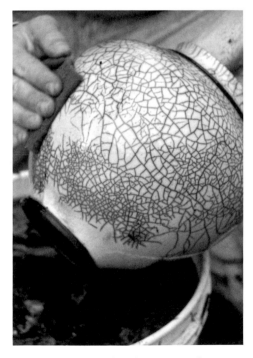

Washing off reduction carbon.

*Andrew Delp, lighthouse and island sculpture
with glass and suspended crystal, 25" tall.*

Epilogue

I hope this book will not only serve further the needs of those who make raku pottery but will also bring information and awareness to those who have not yet attempted the technique.

There is much for the individual to experience and ponder on in raku. The experiences are as much internal as they are external. The interrelatedness of man, material, and process may on occasion give birth to a uniquely beautiful pot and this is good. But that which binds the potter to raku is not a finished pot, anymore than a child is the only thing that binds a man and a woman. It is the accompanying experiences and transformations that serve as a continuous and binding force. A force that is unsummoned. A force that can lead to new acts of artistic expression and ways of living.

It is this formative force that, to me, is characteristic of the raku experience; the resultant pottery is of secondary importance. It is not, therefore, coincidental or ironical to find much of raku pottery infused with an invisible, loving, sensitive, and often imaginative spirit. Awareness is inherent to the realm of raku. If we are aware of the moment, aware of ourselves, we, as well as our pots, will have content.

To be aware and to live with a traveling mind is to bring one's uniqueness to fruition. In this sense the artist today is becoming one of America's modern heroes. In our contemporary heterogeneous society where there are fewer and fewer socially maintained group rites and values they become the new spiritual guides. When individual self-expression is a culturally accepted undertaking, artists, by communicating their own experiences and inner quests, become the new heroes. Their Odyssey, like the adventures of heroes in mythology, embraces change (the hallmark of continuing growth and wholeness). The humanness of their choices and definitions of self, renews commitments of passion and aids today's women and men in their search for meaning. They help us to understand the human spirit and to cherish the freedom to risk; to enjoy the risking as an empowering adventure into self as well as into love, work and - as part of a larger whole - life.

Pottery, ceramics, is a metaphor for life. Because it is just not about what we do but also about who we are, it exists as a nurturing process of personal development as much as it does as a process for making objects. I would hope that you recognize and understand that the object, the finished pot, is secondary to what happens to you inside during its nativity. The creating process has little to do with talent and everything to do with human experience. If we allow ourselves to float into it and to flow with it rather than overly control, manipulate or even battle it, the process can become a freeing experience . . . if not a spiritual practice.

Clay is a powerful vehicle. It can be a healthy, trusting, sharing and playful activity as much as it can be an empty, purposeless, stay-busy activity - the choice is ours in how we choose to commune with it. There are times when we feel despair rather than fulfillment in our work; this is often due to a lack of kinship between material, form and expression. When this happens, pots become just words and not poems. Delight and comfort is taken with "traditional" forms with no search made for poetic ones. As individuals with inherent creative gifts, why do we neglect our passion? Why not sponsor our personal feelings, celebrate our experiences, honor our sacred birth cry?

Clay was freight.
Miracle was the fertilization of dead matter.
Reflection was a provoker.
Vision was a consequence.
Struggle was nourishment.
Invention was fiction.
Independence was ironical.
Eden was technique.
Failure was conceitment.
The SOUL was the hero.
Theme was image.
Craft was breeze.
Tradition a lie.
Respectful attention notwithstanding.
Dialogue with the self, with the clay he made a pot.

Safety
Precautions

Pottery is not a dangerous activity, but as with anything else, accidents can happen if you are not alert to possible hazards, and if you do not employ safety precautions at all times. Accidents can be caused by the nature and condition of the equipment and facilities, or by personal practices, or by both. As a teacher I have always tried to recognize hazards for the purpose of eliminating or minimizing them, and of mollifying their effects. But more importantly, I have come to realize the importance of having a positive attitude toward being safe. If the desire to be safe exists at all times—even during those moments of eagerness inherent to raku pottery—injury can be prevented. Safety, like making good pottery, requires awareness. Many hazards, nevertheless, exist and are included here so that you may be aware of them, and take the necessary preventative precautions. Forewarned is forearmed.

Lead Glazes

The lead base glazes used by many raku potters present a hazard with respect to personal health and safety. If the lead base glazes are frequently used, they should be handled with extreme caution and care should be taken so that the lead, or the lead glaze is not placed on surfaces which might be used, at any time or in any way, for food or drink.

The glaze should not come into contact with your skin and the dust vapors should not be inhaled. This includes the possible inhaling of lead particles that might be circulating in the air from the use of a spray gun, or the particles that might be inhaled while in the vicinity of the kiln flue opening (lead fumes are expelled by lead glazes during the firing).

Lighting the Burner

Burners should be lit the instant the gas is turned on. When lighting the burner, hold it in your hand, and away from the burner port. Should the wind, or some other chance happening cause the burner to go out, the kiln should be purged of any gas before relighting. Remember, propane gas, unlike natural gas, is heavier than air and will cling to the kiln floor and not dissipate immediately by going out of an upper flue.

Kiln Site

Fires also can flare up at the kiln site. They usually come from careless handling of hot fired ware, especially if the kiln is located in a field of dry grass and not in a sandy area. Clear the dry brush and grass from the kiln area before building and firing the kiln.

Exploding Ware Inside the Kiln

If, during the firing, a damp pot should begin to explode, the kiln should be opened and the broken fragments removed before they fuse to other pots. However, do this with extreme caution: sometimes pieces will suddenly come shooting out of the open kiln at a great velocity. Above all, do not look into the peep hole to see what has happened.

Post Firing Reduction

When placing ware in containers for post firing reduction, be on the lookout for possible flame-ups. Combustibles, particularly dry or oil treated sawdust, will ignite instantly on contact with the glowing ware. These combustibles can send up dangerous flames as well as billows of blinding smoke.

EXTRA care should be taken when opening an air-tight reduction container. The inrush of air will, in some cases, re-ignite the combustible material in the bottom of the hole or can, and flames will shoot out.

Respiratory Protection

Anyone involved with the mixing of clays and chemicals, the spraying of glazes, the toxic vaporizing of some chemicals released during firing and the smoke from post-firing reduction should be wearing a NIOSH/MSHA approved respirator. I personally like the inexpensive North brand (7190) welder's disposable/reusable respirator. For maximum protection against organic vapors, fumes, dust, etc., W. W. Grainger, Inc. sells a facepiece that takes two North brand (N7500–83) cartridges. Cartridges, like replacable filters, should be changed when they become difficult to breath through otherwise breathing pressure begins to draw particles through. A respirator should fit properly as well as comfortably. Many companies now make them in various sizes, unfortunately, people with beards, like myself, seem unable to get an adequate fit.

Hair

Long hair is best tied back or tucked under your collar or other clothing at the back of your neck.

Clothing

Loose clothing anywhere can be a problem; I have seen baggy sweater sleeves and baggy pants cuffs catch fire. It is a good idea to have a heavy wool flame retardant fire-blanket nearby and handy whenever you are firing your kiln. If a person's clothing does catch on fire, bring them to the ground with the burning side uppermost. With whatever is at hand smother the flames, directing them away from the head. If alone . . . stop, drop and roll. Do not remove clothing stuck to a burn, cut around it and obtain prompt medical attention.

Bare Feet

Bare feet, like exposed legs or arms, present additional risks for the potter. Shoes and jeans protect the potter from painful and harmful burns.

Sandals should not be worn around the kiln or reduction area. Hot and burning sparks, cinders, or ashes may get caught and trapped between the toes or between the sandals and the feet.

Eyes

Light inside a hot raku kiln can be very intense. Wear infrared-blocking glasses or protective goggles with shade ratings between 1.7 and 3.0 when looking into a glowing kiln. Sunglasses do not offer sufficient protection against infrared radiation.

Hands

To protect the fingers and hands from burns, which frequently come from the irresistible impulse to touch the still-hot pots or kilns, welding gloves are a necessity. When holes burn through the gloves or the gloves wear out, they should be replaced immediately.

Many of my students prefer to own their own pair of protective gloves. Sometimes, as many as twenty students get together and personally place an order to take advantage of a price discount on quantity.

The fourteen inch and the elbow length Red Ram leather glove is both preferred and popular with my students. It is a soft textured, heat resistant leather that is comfortable yet rugged and long lasting. They are available in men's and women's sizes from the Elliott Glove Company in Oconto, Wisconsin, for under twenty dollars. They also offer a line of sleeves and other protective safety clothing made from flame-resistant and self-extinguishing fabrics.

Burns

Nothing but cold water should be put on burns. Immediately immerse the burned area in cold water, or hold it under cold running tap water. Do this for at least ten minutes or longer until the pain lessens or stops. Do not apply ice, lotions or ointments. Superficial burns can be very painful and severe burns (third-degree) relatively painless. Severe burns destroy all the layers of skin and require emergency care at the nearest medical facility.

For those who are alert, hazards can be seen and overcome. Like life, there is no blueprint to safety—one must simply do the best they can, not only for themselves but for everyone.

Marvin Sweet, Beltu's Dance, 20¹/₂″ × 9¹/₂″ × 9¹/₂″.

INSTRUCTIONAL VHS VIDEO CASSETTES

RAKU KILN BUILDING

The first video, of a comprehensive set of three videos, that visually outlines the process of contemporary raku ceramics. This part shows the fabrication of a top loading soft firebrick kiln. Details examined include: the foundation, layout of the floor, bricking of the walls, built-in shelf supports, the burner port, use of target bricks and construction of a liftable, compression brick top complete with flue openings. Seen also, is a homemade natural gas burner with flexible fuel hose, snap-on fittings and a removable forced-air blower unit. Following instructions on the safe lighting of the burner, equally as precise fabrication details are shown for building a fiber blanket kiln with an expanded metal frame. And, for those with access to them, approaches to converting old or unused electric kilns to gas fired raku kilns are explained and displayed. VHS 43 minutes

RAKU FIRING AND REDUCTION

Raku artist and teacher Robert Piepenburg demonstrates his approach to firing raku ceramics: revealing the fascinating dynamics of the post firing reduction process. With a seasoned awareness he explains the theory and the technical aspects behind the sequence of events employed to achieve the glossy richness of a white crackle glaze and to effectively realize the full color spectrum of a "dry" copper surface patina. The intricacies of this ceramic phenomena are so subtle that only a film as fully illuminating as this could enhance the viewer's understanding of current raku practices. Equally rich in primary source material and visual detail it profiles the firing of two kiln loads of work, of significantly different shapes, to demonstrate how various forms might best be reduced after they leave the kiln. Contains coverage of the kiln loading and unloading, lighting the burner, reduction inside the kiln, preparation of combustible materials and the stimulating impact of the smoking applications on the finished pieces themselves. An invaluable supplement to any perspective on raku! VHS 30 minutes

RAKU CLAY GLAZES AND TONGS

A to-the-point demonstration and explanation of how various ingredients can be integrated to formulate handbuilding and wheelthrowing clay bodies capable of withstanding, continuously, the thermo shocks of the raku firing process. Equally as focused coverage is given to glazes. Formulas are shared, chemicals are mixed by volume and a straight forward application of glaze is applied to both traditional and sculptural forms. Through sequential steps of bending and shaping, with common tools, an inexpensive yet practical pair of long handled tongs are formed from flat iron. In total, this definitive film spotlights a number of highly technical and significant ceramic processes that, within a raku context, become an invaluable complement to an expanded overview of information. VHS 33 minutes

BEGINNING WHEELTHROWING

A step-by-step introductory and reference guide to learning the potter's wheel. Visual close-ups of techniques, detailing precise hand and tool positions, balanced with an informal dialogue on expression and form analysis, Piepenburg provides an invaluable supplement to "hands-on" learning. Filmed in a clear and lively style, the visual images and information effectively help viewers to understand and learn wedging, centering, opening, raising the wall, shaping from the cylindrical form, throwing open and closed shapes, trimming right side up, use of throwing ribs and a whole array of other significant fundamentals that enable them to advance their skills in one of the world's oldest yet most contemporary art forming processes. VHS 53 minutes

BEGINNING HANDBUILDING
A stimulating introduction to the basic and innovative ceramic handbuilding techniques including external support molds, internal support molds, stiff slab construction and sectional form fabrication. Following each demonstration, creative forms by various other individuals are shown. While emphasis is on the processes and procedures of construction, a great deal of discussion centers around design, application and sources of inspiration for personal expressions in clay. VHS 56 minutes

SMOKE FIRING
Lays the groundwork for beginning practitioners of simple, primitive fired clay by presenting the basic procedures and follow through of the wood firing of several works, of various shapes, in a reclaimed oil drum. Features clay body selection, clay form recommendations, burnishing, selection of combustibles, placement of pottery, use of salt and copper chemicals for fuming, possible experimental innovations, application of waxes on fired pieces and discusses health and safety issues. By using realistic examples and a nontechnical approach for clarity, beginners are encouraged to proceed from practical tips, trial efforts and possible expectations. VHS 25 minutes

A VISIT WITH THE ARTIST
This videotape focuses on the human dimensions of Robert Piepenburg the artist and presents a personal perspective on ceramics, the creative process and self-empowerment. While working with clay he freely talks about his experiences, beliefs, insights and hopes in ways that engage personal reflection and motivate action. As he intimately shares his own thoughts and as we watch him trustingly explore the experience of his own humanness with the clay, we begin to understand what he means when he says ". . . clay requires resolution through individual uniqueness." VHS 25 minutes

ORDERING INFORMATION
If you would like to purchase any of Robert Piepenburg's videotapes, order autographed copies of his books *Raku Pottery* and *The Spirit Of Clay* or receive information about arranging for workshops please write to: Robert Piepenburg, c/o Pebble Press, 24723 Westmoreland, Farmington Hills, MI 48336–1963

Payment And Mailing Information
Checks or money orders should be in US funds only. Purchase orders will be invoiced. Videotapes are $49.95 each. Shipping and handling charges in the continental US are $2.50 for the first book or cassette and $1.00 for each additional item. For non US and overseas orders, including Alaska and Hawaii, shipping and handling is 25% of the total order. These shipments are sent Parcel Post and may take 4 to 8 weeks.

Photo Credits

All photographs and illustrations by Robert Piepenburg except:

Neil Atkins: 62, 63, 64, 76
David Knox: 126, 127
Michael Gwinup: 35
Richard Wood: 38
Joe Zajac: 18 (top)
Jeff Mincham: cover
Maurice Grossman: 23
Tim Blanchard: 44
Richard Hirsch: 49, 87
Bill Pelletier: 3, (fourth color insert), 20 (bottom), 25, 41, 56 (top), 76, 78, 159
Bill Lemki: 51
Ana England: 53, 54 (top)
Monti Mayrend: 55 (top)
Chou, Pang-Ling: 55 (bottom), (third color insert)
Steve Wieneke: 56 (bottom), (fourth color insert, bottom), 20 (top)
Chris Thompson: 57 (top)
Rafael A. Duran: 57 (bottom)
Jeremy Jernegan: 100 (bottom), 101 (bottom)
Steve Myers: 58
Jerry L. Caplan: 69 (bottom)
Ed Risak: 73
Ko-on: 43
Morse Collection, Museum of Fine Arts, Boston: 37, 45
Sandor B. Brent: 46
Sister Celeste Mary Bourke: 48
Dave Hines: 71
Gail Piepenburg: (first color insert)
Nancy Selvin: (first color insert, bottom)
Garth Clark Gallery (fourth color insert, top)
John Bonath: 116

E.G. Schempf: (second color insert, top)
Jim Connell: (second color insert, bottom)
Peter Kuentzel: (third color insert)
MMG Photography: (second color insert, bottom)
Paul Soldner: 29, 31, 54 (bottom), 103
Macario: 104
Hank Murrow: 113
Ken Kang: 117
Frank Kulasiewicz: 108 (bottom)
Steven Kemenyffy: 21
Steve Olszewski: 74
Seattle Art Museum: 18 (bottom)
Oakland Community College, Orchid Ridge Campus: 102 (top), 112, 142 (top)
Mark Emmons: 79
Dave Roberts: 14, 86
Patrick Hilferty: 88
Michael Hough: 105
John Martin: 130
Ellen Branfman: 97
John Murphy: 102 (bottom)
Dave and Boni Deal: 105
Jay Redmond: 108
Peneloope Fleming: 125 (top), (second color insert, top)
Georcia Pozycinski: 125 (bottom)
Rachel Porter: 147
Gene Ogami: 26
Daniel Rhodes: 40
Kurt Weiser: (first color insert)
Charles Mayer: 156
Paul Kodama: 142
Rick Webb: 143